THERE ARE NO FLOWERS HERE

COLLECTED LETTERS OF JACK RICHARDSON

MY FAT FOX LTD MMXIV

http://www.myfatfox.co.uk
My Fat Fox Ltd
86 Gladys Dimson House
London
E7 9DF
United Kingdom

FIRST PAPERBACK EDITION 2014
© My Fat Fox 2014

Transcribed from the original handwritten letters by Elizabeth Holloway.

Cover design by Paul Holloway from an original photo of Jack Richardson.

ISBN 978-1-905747-29-0

CONTENTS

To Elizabeth Holloway, without whose patience and persistence this book would not exist

PART ONE
INTRODUCTION

JACK AND MAY

In 1913 John 'Jack' Richardson was the 20 year-old son of the headmaster of Shaftesbury Road Elementary School in Forest Gate, East London. Jack was a lover of the countryside, a talented artist and a linguistics scholar; he adored Beowulf, and quoted Robert Louis Stevenson and Omar Khayyam. May Larby, 18, was the daughter of a local police constable; she was a sharp-minded mathematician with a great thirst for all knowledge, cultural as well as abstract. After a chance meeting on an underground train these two brilliant young people began a doomed love affair.

Jack was one of the many millions of young men who were soon to die in the First World War[1]. Before his death Jack wrote letters to May from his training camp, from his French billets and ultimately from the trenches. These letters, a short essay, a poem and some excerpts from May's memoirs tell their tragic story. Many letters are mundane, but reveal the slow development of Jack and May's relationship, and include fascinating historical details of everyday life at that time. Some later letters are beautifully descriptive of Jack's surroundings, as you might expect from a linguistics scholar, others are painfully poignant when read with the hindsight that Jack did not survive the war to live into old age with his lover as they hoped and expected.

Wherever possible I have provided footnotes to explain references that might appear obscure. In some cases (despite my

---

[1]Over 40 million casualties resulted, including approximately 20 million military and civilian deaths.

best efforts) I have been unable to decipher their meaning. Some may be army slang and others may be personal references that inevitably defy interpretation. If any reader can throw any light on these, an explanatory note written to the publisher at the address given at the beginning of the book would be very welcome.

Grammar and spelling errors have mostly been retained, as they are partly a part of the idiom of the time; Jack's use of "musn't" instead of "mustn't" for example.

This volume means a lot to me personally; May was my maternal grandmother, and her daughter, my mother, Elizabeth Holloway (who died in 2004), spent many hours mastering unfamiliar technology to transcribe the letters. This was not an easy task by any means, as Jack's longhand can be hard to decipher in places. Unfortunately, at the time she was unable to find a publisher; I am pleased to be able to put that to rights now.

By pure coincidence I live in Forest Gate, only a few minutes' walk from where Jack and May lived, nearly a century ago. Treading the same streets they trod, I often think of them, and cast myself back in time in my imagination, so it seems appropriate that I should be finally editing and publishing these letters. I feel sure that Jack, May and my mother Elizabeth would approve.

My thanks to my brother Steve for his support and assistance in putting this book together.

Paul Holloway
Forest Gate
April 2014

FROM THE MEMOIRS OF MAY LARBY

One unforeseen outcome of my attendance at intercollegiate lectures arose from a chance encounter on the underground train that took me to King's College for a morning session, in 1913. I found myself in a very crowded coach sitting diagonally opposite to Jack Richardson, whom I have already mentioned as the son of the Headmaster of my elementary school and a contemporary at Grammar school. I had heard that he was a student in the English Department at King's but as we had had no personal conversation I had forgotten this fact. We exchanged faint smiles of recognition through the gaps among the standing passengers.

When the crowd began to thin and a seat next to him fell vacant, while the seats next to me remained occupied, I realised that we were both bound for the same destination. My natural impulse has always been to make some friendly overture of anyone whom I encountered personally and on this occasion I crossed the compartment to the empty seat and offered the conversational 'Mr Richardson?' I was immediately welcomed by name and an important friendship had started. My lecture at King's was a weekly event and subsequent meetings with Jack were not by chance.

I came to expect to see Jack waiting on the station platform ready to continue our discussions on poetry, social conditions, human motives and the many topics that have concerned students over the centuries. One discovery that mattered profoundly to me was Jack's absorbing interest in the visual arts. In this realm I was almost ignorant though I had enjoyed art lessons in school and from early childhood had been much moved by natural beauty. Jack painted with considerable skill in watercolours and he was familiar with the works of the great painters and sculptors. Now he had an eager pupil and I had a guide to the visual arts; fortunately one who was glad that I already had a guide to music.

Our first visit together was to the Wallace Collection in Manchester Square, a good choice because of its wide range of exhibits. I still remember our arguments over Impressionism and the more mundane fact that we stayed all day without noticing that we had had neither food nor drink.

There were three other well-remembered days spent with Jack Richardson. On one occasion we visited Westminster Abbey. We explored every nook and cranny, delighting in both beauty and history. Subsequent ceremonial visits have only strengthened my early sense that for me this was the expression of the Christian faith in England.

Another day was spent at the church of St Bartholomew the Great in Smithfield, a place of regal simplicity which has since for me been linked with a related foundation, the hospital of the same name where my son took his medical training. The third church to which I was introduced was a near neighbour of King's College, the Temple Church, whose setting next to the lawns which run down to the Thames Embankment gives a wonderful backdrop to its history.

The companionship of my two male guides meant more to me than my friendships with the women of my college, not for any sexual implications but because they had so much more experience of human living. Ted was the European representative of a firm which sold graphite as a lubricant alternative to oil; he kept me in touch with affairs in Western Europe as well as with music and its history. Jack had a deep knowledge of the English countryside gleaned from his paintings of scenes in East Anglia and its churches. In comparison, my fellow students' narrow sheltered lives gave me little stimulus, though I came to admire some of them profoundly for the great courage they showed in the tragic years that lay shrouded in the future....

For two years my friendship with Jack Richardson had been growing with a deepening level of common interests. We met frequently, at his house or mine, alone in the room set aside for study. We talked chiefly of books and literary commentary, the poetry of our day and the English Review, the novels of Thomas Hardy and H.G. Wells, the views of Bernard Shaw, Bertrand Russell and leading politicians. But I became uneasy as I realised how much of my time and thought was related to Jack; I was restless if we did not happen to meet; I looked for an excuse to call on him, to return a book perhaps. I was anxious if he did not arrange to take me to some interesting place. By midsummer 1914 my proud self-sufficiency felt threatened; I was becoming dependent on the responses of another being! I told of my misgivings and proposed a month's voluntary abstinence; we would not meet during that time. Reluctantly and sceptically he agreed; he saw no harm in our mutual dependence!

In fact, well before the end of the scheduled month I had capitulated; I missed his companionship so acutely and so constantly that I had to confess that I was unbearably miserable without it and could not endure the deprivation. We realised face to face that we were in love and we sealed the confession with our first kiss. This gentle simple act was deeply significant to me.

Although my family was closely knit, physical demonstrations of affection were discouraged. I had hitherto known only the formal kiss of greeting or goodbye that was expected of relatives. This new physical contact was a very different symbol. It expressed a bond of mutual interests, companionship and romantic love that seemed the very basis of living. It foreshadowed the deepest personal relationship, the greatest happiness and the keenest anguish of my long life.

My plans now seemed to be taking a foreseeable shape. When my degree had been achieved I would apply to the Essex Authority for an extension of my grant so that I could take a year's course of postgraduate training for teaching. I expected then to find a congenial post in a grammar school where mathematics was regarded as an important subject. Marriage would presumably follow a few years later. Jack wanted to continue his linguistic studies and vaguely looked forward to University work of some kind. We had no foreboding of any deterioration in our circumstances. Such problems as low wages, unemployment and strikes seemed curable; we believed confidently in the inevitability of Progress. Besides we were proudly aware of our Empire, our authority as the leading world power, our command of the oceans. It was a period of patriotism with its Empire Day and such songs as 'Rule, Britannia'; we had a sense of mission, but it was to other countries.

Within the last two or three years there had been war scares in the Press; and we had read Erskine Childer's 'Riddle of the Sands'. We thought these over-dramatised! I relied more on reports of unrest in some continental countries from Ted Moody who knew the industrial cities well. Unexpectedly I learned something of the situation in Russia from three engineers studying here whom I had been asked to help with their English. In the course of their group lessons they told me about their own experiences of the abortive rising of 1905, the persecution of the Jews and the current opposition to the Czar's regime. This stimulated an interest in Russia which has been fully developed in recent years.

Great Britain did not seem involved in any of these troubles. Nevertheless the slogan of the day was 'Be prepared'. The young responded: I joined the college Voluntary Aid Detachment and learned something about nursing the possible overseas wounded; Jack joined the University Officer Training Corps and in the second half of July 1914 he was on Salisbury Plain camping with his detachment.

Then came the eruption of violence in Serbia, and the chain of alliances led to a real threat of military action by Britain. Jack's group were asked to volunteer for service; he immediately gave his name. All this seemed unreal until Germany's army entered Belgium and broke the international agreement to respect the integrity of smaller countries. Britain issued an ultimatum, as Jack's detachment knew on Salisbury Plain. Suddenly we were at war; camp was struck; Jack came home and very soon was commissioned in the City of London Regiment with headquarters in Westminster. Weeks of recruiting and training followed; orders for transfer to overseas postings were given, then cancelled; and the battle news became very grave. Trench lines were drawn and the casualty figures became horrifying.

Meanwhile I, at home, felt my life split in two. One part was spent with Jack in his new exacting role; the other was taken up with the study of abstract mathematical entities such as quaternions.

But I duly achieved a fairly satisfactory degree (an upper second, which was thought creditable for a 19-year-old) and was given a grant for professional training which was to start at Bedford College Education Department in January 1915.

May Williams (née Larby)

PART TWO
LETTERS FROM ENGLAND

296 Katherine Road,
Forest Gate, E.7.
21/7/13

Dear Miss Larby,

I was pleased to get your letter this morning. I thank you for your good wishes and rejoice to hear you have seen Haddon Hall[2]. I have not; but I have heard of its glories, of its ovens which, I'm told, cook bullocks whole, and the like. You will come back, doubtlessly, a compleat philosopher and an optimist of redoubled strength, content to dream for every moment that the "grass is green". I hope you like the bagpipes. I, and my musical taste, you know, is of the most doubtful, am very fond of them. Among the hills I should think they must be fine.

But why do you add "- of course" to the statement about the rowdiness of the men? And you were patient onlookers too! "Grisilde is dead and hiere pacience"[3], you know. You must remember the records of Holloway and rejoice[4]; but in the matter of rowdiness, I am sure you look down on us from

---

[2]A mediaeval manor house and home of the Dukes of Rutland, the Manners family, in the Peak District alongside the River Wye near Bakewell, Derbyshire.

[3]"Grisilde is deed, and eek hire pacience.", meaning "Griselda's dead, and dead is her patience." Geoffrey Chaucer 'The Canterbury Tales'. .

[4]This reference, to "the records of Holloway", is unclear but probably refers to Holloway College.

heights we never reached. Learn Gaelic, even if you miss the doctrine! In the South your reputation for learning will then mount to giddy heights; you will understand the subtleties of Mr.Yeats[5]. "It's a consummation devoutly to be wished"[6]!

The opening of your new buildings has, I see, brought rebuke upon you; you steal the peoples' land, five acres of it! Are you not a Socialist?

I am going to Benfleet next Wednesday, for a week, to waste paint and paper, and then back to work until October, after which I may cheerfully "damn the consequences".

Yours Sincerely,

J. E. Richardson

296, Katherine Road

Forest Gate E.7.

21.11.13

Dear May,

Of course it is not true; you are "fed up" with this matter you write about and you are worrying over work. I know what the second is; it occurred, as I think I've told you, every Wednesday, after I had seen Guthkelch[7]; but it is silly, I know now, for after

---

[5]William Butler Yeats was born 1865 in Dublin, Ireland. While he never learned Gaelic himself, his poetry is full of references to Irish mythology and folklore.

[6]Hamlet, act 3, sc. 1, l. 62-3. "consummation" meaning 'death'.

[7]Jack's English lecturer

all, the work does not really matter to the extent of a worked example.

I have written; and that's enough; I hope it is the end of the business as far as you are concerned.

The dropping of name-handles is fine; I wanted to do it but had not the initiative. In making friends I am no good; in all probability I should have not known you now beyond a "good morning" had you not fortunately spoken first.

I have not started your sketch, but I shall, and will deliver the two with the "English Reviews"[8] even before the month is out.

Jack Richardson

296, Katherine Road

Forest Gate E.7.

11.12.13

Dear May,

I had read "Marriage"[9], taken it back and herewith send you the ticket and am not a penny the worse off for funds. I am sending the ticket instead of making it an excuse to call, because I appeared last Sunday night and once in a week is quite often enough for me to disturb you. This is not an excuse because I

---

[8]Journal of early 20th-century English-language literature, founded by Ford Madox Ford in 1908.

[9]'Marriage' a novel by H.G. Wells (1913).

won't or don't want to, but a well considered reason which you should appreciate.

I thought the book splendid, especially Marjorie Trafford did not seem to me so living a character; but rather a number of persons, used partly to illustrate M. and partly to expound Wells, but still jolly interesting. Mr Pope is the personification of Middle Age.

Next Wednesday morning at 9.30 on Upton Park[10] will suit, I suppose. I seem to remember you said so the other evening.

    Jack

I should have thanked you for the loan above.

296, Katherine Road

Forest Gate E.

Dear May,

I was sorry to hear you were ill this morning; I hope you are already better. It was good of you to let me know and I owe Norman[11] my best thanks. Our outing, then, is still an anticipated pleasure instead of a memory only. I shall return the books of yours tomorrow, Wednesday, evening and hope to hear you are well and ready to go quite soon. You should be in no

---

[10]Upton Park underground station, on the District Line, located on Green Street, about 10 minute's walk from Lansdown Road and Katherine Road.
[11]Norman was May's younger brother.

way bothered or hindered as you have been already too much.

Jack

296, Katherine Road
Forest Gate E.

Dear May,

I have been suddenly reminded of the fact that I had arranged to keep house on Wednesday night and so I cannot bring the sketches etc.; the former, I am relieved to say, are finished. Can you come and see me on that evening instead, sometime after 7.30? Before then I shall be acting as a sort of general valet. However, don't trouble to answer whether you can, can't or won't. If you do not appear I shall leave the things on Thursday afternoon.

On Friday may come the result and I have therefore some sort of sickness at heart; it is the unknown even more than the ill-known which causes it.

Jack R.

296, Katherine Road
Forest Gate E.
24.12.13

Dear May,

I returned this afternoon, and so am in time to send you greetings for the Season, and wish you the very best of luck and health for the year to come, especially for the end of next

13

October.

    Jack

P.S. Whatever you do, go away; the country is positively finer now than in the summer and i'faith I left it unwillingly.

296, Katherine Road

Forest Gate.E.

8.1.14.

    Dear May,

I was very pleased indeed to get your letter, for East Ham seems lonely when you are away, and there is none to talk to. "Quomodo sedet sola sivitas"[12] you know. It is very good of you to say I have been, and am, of some use to you, and I am proud of it; but in reality it is I who have the best of the bargain. Your friendship has given me a great deal which I should never otherwise have had and I have spent some pleasant hours with you which I shall not quickly forget. You know I had no-one before I knew you, whom I could talk to as I do to you and who would talk back.

That I like Hardy and you don't is no reason why our temperaments should clash; and they certainly don't for we don't quarrel often, do we? I do not like his fickle men or shallow women any more than you; and Hardy does not mean you should. But Giles is not fickle or poor in spirit, and you

---

[12]Latin - "How doth the city sit solitary"."Quomodo sedet sola civitas' are the first words of the Lamentations of Jeremiah in the Latin translation (the Vulgate Bible).

must remember "The Woodlanders" is a tragedy. It tells of the waste of the good in the world, the sacrifice of the Winterbournes and such as the sparmaker's daughter for the sake of Doctor's race of men.

Hardy's view of people and things is not different from yours or mine, but he is concerned in lamenting the losses of good while you are intent upon its triumphs. In short you are an optimist, heart and soul, he, a pessimist; and though a pessimist sees so much bad, he likes it none the better. I do not think you would quarrel with Hardy any more than with me, his humble disciple! Moreover, there is no cynicism in a book that ends with such an epitaph as does "The Woodlanders" - "He was a good man and did good deeds," it is of the same genre as "King Lear". But please forgive this prosing.

I am glad you find the country so splendid at this time of year, it seemed magnificent to me just before Xmas. Couldn't we have a day in the country, you and I, sometime later? We could have a splendid talk and no times or hours to worry us, with an unending picture gallery as well.

I find the chapels in Westminster are only open free to the public on Mondays and Tuesdays. On other days one must be taken round in a party by a verger who repeats more or less interesting matter by rote. That would not suit us, would it? The only other places I can think of are the Guildhall Gallery and the Victoria and Albert Museum, though there is no reason why we should not see the rest of the Tate pictures. An afternoon will be just long enough. If I don't see you before Thursday you must write and let me know your decision and the place and time of meeting and lunch.

You know, May, if I came to see you as often as I wanted to, it would be disastrous for your work and might wear out your patience. I come to see you, therefore, not as often as I want to, but no more often than I think I ought; but it is awfully good of you to ask me as you do, and I appreciate it and be assured "will think it wise".

This is the longest letter I have ever written and would pray you remember it is my first offence and forgive me accordingly.

Yours,

Jack

296, Katherine Road
Forest Gate E.
Sunday

Dear May,

I have had a fit of restlessness and "blue devils" this week and week-end and so I am writing to you again. Of your charity I hope you will consent to be bored.

On Friday afternoon I went to an agency as I told you I was going to, and recited all the qualifications I could muster. I was prepared to teach, as well as English, Latin and History to B.A. pass standard, and all other arts subjects for Matric! Drawing certificates were quoted, and I was ready to hold forth on Antiquities if necessary. Vacancies are to be sent me and I live in hopes.

Yesterday afternoon I spent in Hyde Park drilling in sweat and sunshine. However, it counts two drills. Today I have been painting at Lambourne End[13] and I am not overpleased with the result. You will see that work was an "also ran".

By the way, I came across an interesting account of a terrible dragon born and bred in "St. Leonard's Forest" near Horsham. It, I mean the account, was printed in 1610 and seems to have caused a stir at the time. If I remember, Horsham has degenerated to boarhounds since then.

Another note; in a review of Maurice Hewlett's "Mrs. Lancelot", the author is said to have been a great reader of Meredith[14] and to have been much influenced in all his work by him. I had not thought of it had you?

May you will come out with me for a day at the end of term? After these three weeks of work you will be at peace with yourself and sessionals will be over. This residence will be worth any amount to you for "final"; and you don't think any thing about cracking up now, do you?

May, dear, you were good to write as you did last week and I appreciate it. I think you will be able to come and see me again without feeling that Mother is between us. I hope you will; I shall miss so much if you come only as an ordinary visitor.

Please forgive this rigmarole; it is a relief to write to you.

> Yours,
>
> Jack

---

[13]A picturesque location in Essex.
[14]George Meredith (1828–1909).

296, Katherine Road,
Forest Gate E.
31.3.14.

Dear May,

Thanks very much for your letter and congratulations on going away into the country. The gods work for you in spite of your wilfulness, care for you more than you do for yourself and in the person of your sister whisk you into the paths you should go along. You should be very grateful to your sister who I hope will be the better for the rustication.

I am sorry I have got the "Open Road", it ought to be in Sussex on a morning like this. But you have the actual thing and must leave me the mirror.

I miss a great deal of pleasure in not having your company this week but I shall be repaid by seeing you fit; and if the weather is like it is this morning I shall have a double share of sunshine at Abridge, one lot direct from the sky, the other reflected from Sussex hills.

I have no excuse for slacking now, for the original edition of Warner which Dr. Gollanz promised me came this morning and only waits to be used. As for the work you are doing now, it will be worth hours done last term and is the sort which leads to firsts. You must do well in the Final, get a first in spite of Hilton to glorify impulse and your enthusiasm.

I shall work well this week in anticipation of next and when I think how little we knew each other last Easter, and what your friendship means to me this, there is no room, May, but for optimism, at least for the present. "Let us eat and drink and be merry for tomorrow we die!"[15]

Yours,

Jack

296, Katherine Road,
Forest Gate E.
2.4.14

Dear May,

I shall be only too pleased to meet you at London Bridge on Saturday evening. It is very good of you to ask me. I have nothing on and in spite of your "only if's" it would make little difference if I had.

It's a good sign that you are hurrying with your work, you cannot be tired now, at any-rate.

I think you are right about the cruel, distant gods,

> "as flies to wanton boys are we to the gods;
> they kill us for their sport"[16].

Our fellows are worth much more gratitude.

No, May, what ever optimism I may have is not independent of your influence. I will not agree that my quotation is morbid; it may be gloomy but I have not renounced pessimism. The

---

[15]This is an odd hybrid Biblical quote. The first part is from Ecclesiastes (8:15) the second part from Isaiah (22:13).

[16]King Lear, William Shakespeare.

19

beauty of Nature and the World may be part of its cruelty, to blind us for the time to the inevitable blows and pain. Do you remember the poem in the "English Review"? But all this is for the sake of argument for I feel anything but gloomy and Spring came into the garden yesterday.

I hope you regard whist with the requisite seriousness; remember Mrs. Battle and treat it with becoming decorum. At such times there must be nothing but "a clean hearth and the rigour of the game"[17].

I am glad your sister is better and please thank her for me.

> Yours,
>
> Jack

P.S. I cannot call you Katherine because of your letter and the fact that it never suits you. Pallas Athena stands for wisdom and valour alone and is therefore incomplete; I must rest unrevenged.

> 296, Katherine Road
> Forest Gate E.
> 20.4.14.

Dear May,

You are right, absolutely right, and you show me why with a courage and kindness of which I think only you are capable. I could not understand before. You see I thought you were going

---

[17] From "Mrs. Battle's Opinions on Whist" by Charles Lamb.

to turn our friendship into an acquaintanceship, that we were gradually to drift apart and become strangers. I feared you meant to smash my splendid and only coloured window as a trial of strength, and I could not lose such a possession without a struggle. Now you have made everything clear, and not only have you left me my window but made it more splendid than before.

Of course you must have quiet to concentrate on your work. Your Final must be your only goal now. Yours is the only method to escape from the flatness of life which causes unrest, and now whatever happens you must be at peace with yourself. You are right, our friendship has been anything but calm, or at least only calm on the surface, and such an influence is dead against Final work. I should have realized this before. The only way to stop such a disturbing current is to break the contact, and, just as electricity, the old current will flow again when the contact is re-established. It will be hard but we must do it, May; and you say that it need be a temporary break only. If ever I was in debt to you I am now, and the very least I can do is to help you all I can now you need it most.

 May, you are in nothing mad but marvellously sane and strong. I will try to equal you in the latter; but for my peace of mind you must promise never to suspect indifference. The less I cared the less careful should I be to follow your wishes which I am convinced are thoroughly right.

    Jack

296, Katherine Road,
Forest Gate E.

Dear May,

Now I am alone I realise what a hard task you have given me or
I have given myself. There must be a great difference in our
friendship, but I will try to make it concern me only. You will see
that memories will make the endeavour somewhat painful at
first, and if I do not altogether succeed to begin with you must
have patience until I have in part learnt it.

Jack

King's College,
Strand W.
11.6.14

Dear May,

Thank you so much for your letter. You are very good to me and
very generous. Nothing could have hurt me more than to think
my mother, of all people, should be the one to cause you pain
and put a barrier between us. You and mother must understand
one another and when you do I am certain you will be friends. I
care for you both too much for you to be any thing else.

I have no right to be cross with you and much cause to be
grateful. May, it would be a great cause that would separate us
now. I want to see you and talk to you, not to write.

Yours,

Jack

296, Katherine Road,
Forest Gate E.

Tuesday

Dear May,

What has happened that I did not meet you at 1 o'clock today? I was there before my time so I cannot have missed you. I went on to University College to see if you turned up for your 3 o'clock lecture.

Not seeing you, I got worried. I did not write last night as you said in your letter that I was to let you know if I could not come. Needless to say I was disappointed; anyhow let me know if you are alright etc. and then perhaps I can meet you another day.

Yours,

Jack

296, Katherine Road,
Forest Gate E.

Dear May,

I have just found that there are two Marylebone churches; I suppose I waited at the wrong one, i.e. St. Marylebone. I am awfully sorry to have given you the trouble of waiting in vain.

May I see you on Wednesday morning at Baker Street station to apologise? At any rate I shall be there at 9.30 and wait till 10 o'clock in case I may. If you are not there in the ordinary way between those times please don't alter your arrangements; I deserve to be punished for my carelessness.

Jack

296, Katherine Road,
Forest Gate E.
26.6.14.

Dear May,

I am glad you have talked to Hilton and I hope you have cut today. You must be careful now, you know, and sessionals are not worth being ill over. It's a jolly good thing you have Ted to look after you. It will be splendid for you to go to Richmond with him; and you will go out on Sunday too, won't you? You mustn't crock up now, May, besides it would be hard luck on Hilton. I should think port the medicine of medicines.

Do you know, dear, I can't squeeze out a decent idea for Monday. We ought to go where it's quiet and peaceful; but you are in the middle of London and I don't know anything about the country on the other side. The only place I can think of is St. Albans, but you have just been there and so it will not be fresh to you. If you want a day in London we can leave the arrangements until I meet you on Monday morning at Baker Street station at 11.15. If you have any suggestion please let me know. As long as I am with you, May, I don't care where we go; but we may as well have the place in harmony with your feelings which means it will be with mine also.

I am sorry I was so depressing and dull on Monday. I am not often rude to you in that way and you must forgive me this once. You know you did tantalise me over that house on fire, though I pretended indifference at the time. I find I cannot go past there now without thinking of you on a passing motorbus!

Why do you suggest I should mind you going to Richmond on Friday? May my dear, even if I had any right to mind, which I have not, don't you know that I admire you too much to be so childish?

On Tuesday Guthkelch, the English lecturer, gave me the name of a Russian professor who wants two hours English conversation a day for three months. I have applied for the job. Guthkelch suggested I should ask half a crown an hour. That's thirty shillings a week, eighteen pounds for the three months; I hope I get it!

The lecture by Gilbert Murray was splendid. He derived Hamlet from the Winter God of primitive myths. I must tell you about it on Monday.

You will see from the tone of this letter and its length that I am no longer peevish. I hope you are already bucking up in spite of these three pages. Have a good time on Friday and go out with Ted on Sunday; there must be no getting homesick and depressed now.

Yours,

Jack

296, Katherine Road,
Forest Gate E.
16.7.14.

My dear May,

Thank you so much for your letter. I have hated the flippancy and unreality which has come between us as much as you have. We must not have this fresh barrier between us, dear; it has been hard enough to break down the first. I do hope you will gain peace and more serenity during this long vac. Your present state of unrest and worry is wearing you out.

 I want to be with you alone; just we two with no-one to disturb us. We can talk then, and that will be so much better than writing May, dear. I think we shall find it easy to fall back into the old comradeship, and there is that between us now that should make it so much more splendid. Don't let us be shy and half ashamed of ourselves and our feelings.

I will call this evening to hear when we can go out together and talk.

> Yours,
>
> Jack

Windmill Hill Camp,
University of London O.T.C[18].
Ludgershall,
Wiltshire
Sunday

---

[18]Officer Training Corps - The critical shortage of officers during the South African War (1899-1902) led to the establishment in 1908 of an Officer Training Corps as part of the Haldane Reforms.

26

Dear May,

I have more time today than I am like to have any time in the week so I write now to be on the safe side and give you no excuse for not answering. The C.U.[19] provide large tents for writing and reading so we can write and pray in comfort. The camp is perched on the slope of a hill on the very edge of Salisbury Plain, and standing on the top you can see the ring of cultivated country all around and the edge of the stretch of grass which extends away for miles. In the distance are ridge after ridge and the sides are splendidly wooded. In the evening and early morning they are all shades of blue. Last night the evening sky was splendid, changing from delicate pinks to gorgeous orange and red, and the black storm clouds made it more beautiful by contrast.

The village of Ludgershall is old world and I think very interesting. There are the remains of a market cross and a splendid church, Norman, with additions of all periods. Opposite is an ancient inn, last night filled to overflowing. The interior is full of narrow passages and small low rooms and most of it is panelled. All the back too is what was once a coaching yard with long stables on three sides.

Last night the wind was high and lying in the tent with the flapping of the canvas was weird but pleasant enough.

We seem to be miles from everywhere; Salisbury is the nearest town of any size and that is 11 miles away and the trains there

---

[19]Christian Union

are awkward. I'm afraid we shall not be able to get there and I did want to go. There is one thing that is really splendid, the cider. There are barrels of it and it is so easy to get thirsty here.

Last night when it was dark and just the points of tents showed up against the sky line which was still faintly coloured, and the few lamps were lit to show the lines, the place looked mysterious and peaceful. To add to the effect the drum and fife band paraded the camp and the wail of fifes could be heard a mile or two away.

The inside of the canteen provided a fine contrast. It is brilliantly lighted with acetylene lamps and barrels of beer piled up at the ends. In the centre, last night, sat a circle of medicals singing an endless ditty on the glories of the Medicals O.T.C.

> "There's none so fair
> As can compare
> With the medical O.T.C..."

runs the chorus; the rest is often unquotable.

You will see, May, from the length of this epistle that it's a "first copy". In an ordinary way I should cut, trim and condense it down to a page and a half. But you asked for it, you know, so you must forgive its dullness and length. Besides I feel slack and fuddled this morning. No, it was not cider last night.

Goodbye, dear, work well, but not too hard and keep "bucked". You looked so well on Friday, look so when I come back.

Jack

University of London O.T.C.

B Coy,

Windmill Hill Camp,

Ludgershall,

Wiltshire.

Dear May,

I got your letter from the Orderly Corporal in the "lines". I was very glad to get it and you do write well, you know.

I will not admit I was necessarily an optimist over the ships passing in the night. I never suggested they would go on sailing for ever, that they would not sink, or worse, be drawn up, one at one time one at another, high and dry on some low mud-flat, to rot in the wind and sun. As I have said before, May, I am not of Hardy's type of pessimism but follow R.L.S[20]. I will admit the final failure of things in death and lack of accomplishment, but there are some splendid things in life and the voyage together is the most splendid of all. Then "Let us eat, drink and be merry for tomorrow we die".

May, dear, you are right about the necessity for my going out among men and women and growing older; but I will not agree that it is necessary for me to test my estimate of you. You do not choose your comrade as you would pick out a ripe fat plum by comparing it with greener and smaller ones. I have come to care for you by a process subtler than that. It is by knowing you well that I come to be sure that I want your comradeship more than anything else. Though I am sure I can not make anyone

---

[20]Robert Louis Stevenson

else convinced in the same manner, and that is why I must go out into the world and grow older and mature. From the first your personality attracted me and this instinctive feeling is not to be strengthened by comparing you with others, but by knowing you even better. By all means let me know the world better, but it shall be a training for me, not a test for you who, since I care for you so much, I must be certain I need it not.

I can well understand your feelings while you were at Wanstead[21]. This is not the first time you have been affected like this by the Westlakes, but never so strongly before.

I am having a really good time here and the weather is just cool enough for field work and the like. This morning we had a combined attack up a high ridge and it meant rushing over a mile up hill in short dashes of a hundred yards. It lasted over three hours and if this doesn't make me fit nothing will.

A curious touch is given to the place by the number of army biplanes continually passing over. Here is a place almost untouched by the last fifty years of civilization and yet the very latest mechanical advances are at their best. So it comes that aeroplanes are more common than trains.

The regularity of the life, inspections, parades, drills and field operations, has the effect of breaking off the flow of ordinary life and it seems literally months since I came here. I have seen no books or papers since Saturday and have only heard of war and rumours of war. By the way, the present crisis in Europe has added a touch of vividness to Camp, for the Commanding

---

[21]Wanstead is a small town north of Forest Gate.

Officer has told us that in the event of the British Army mobilizing we shall be expected to supply three hundred volunteers.

You were not silly on Friday; but I am glad you are still well and not getting tired and worn as you were the previous weeks. Pen's letter and Miss Honeybourn's visit will help to keep you so, I hope, until I come back and long after.

    Jack

P.S. There is a falling off here May; this is not a "first copy".

London University O.T.C
Windmill Hill Camp,
Ludgershall,
Wilts
Sunday

Dear May,

The Adjutant called us up this morning and asked for volunteers in either the Special Reserve or Territorial Force, as subalterns. If mobilization takes place the Camp will be broken up; it may end tomorrow. This would mean we should be called up for training probably next week. I have put my name down for the Territorials. The National Reserve is liable to service abroad, the Territorials not; but if I am in the Territorials I can join the special Imperial Section for foreign service when necessary. I do not know enough yet to be accepted in National Reserve and I do not like to sign on for it until I have seen

Mother and Father.

Of course all this is as yet only provisional and nothing definite can be done until mobilization takes place.

I am writing this in the Guard Tent after having mounted guard since four o'clock yesterday. There are eleven of us in the tent and all talking, so if this is only partially intelligible you will understand.

Yours

Jack

See the magazine clipping among the illustrations, which has the quotation, "Remains without a rival". On the back of the clipping is written:

Dear May,

I saw this in a shop as I came up this morning and so I sent it to you.

Under the quotation on the title page I would write "So shall it not be with us", dear.

Jack

2nd. City of London Royal Fusiliers,
Tattenham Corner,

Epsom.

Dear May,

Everything here is splendid and there has been no trouble at all. We see very little of the Colonel and Major Hogan is practically O.C.. The officers are splendid fellows and I expect a good time. Please excuse scrap of paper - can get no note. Letter later.

Jack

Head Quarters,
Tattenham Corner,
Epsom.
26.2.15.
Friday evening.

My dear,

At last I've got a minute or two to write and some notepaper. I have actually started work, am posted to a Company and second in Command. At present I'm in command, my Captain, a jolly decent fellow, has gone to town and left me with a pile of papers and passes and I don't know what - all to be answered or given out and I don't know what.

The other officers here are jolly decent fellows and keen - the men are the worst I've ever seen - some are almost cripples and some I think mentally deficient, still I suppose there are enough decent ones to go on with. Since I'm alone with the company I can't come home this weekend but I hope the next week. I am starting to learn to ride tomorrow morning in a riding school near by - bareback and hands behind the back - I'm told you are

33

oftener off than on, but my neck is quite strong. How are you? Please send me some paintings and an account of yourself and your doings. And Friday afternoon and tea went well? You are going to see Raphael tomorrow afternoon, n'est ce pas?

It won't be long now, dear, before Leith Hill - a day like yesterday or today will be more than splendid. Do you know I expect to get £20 more kit allowance - enough for an antique silver ring!

I've got lots more to say but no time to say it until Sunday when another letter.

I do look forward to a week tomorrow - you and I, my love -

    Goodbye,

    Jack

Head Quarters,
9 Tufton Street,
Westminster, S.W
Thursday night.

My dear,

I don't know for certain even yet when I shall be going to Epsom, but I think it will be next Monday or Tuesday.

I couldn't write before because I didn't know your address and I haven't been able to get home until tonight to look it up from one of the letters you wrote before from Horsham.

You ought to be having a good time and be ever so much better, especially if you have not broken your determination to do no work for the first week.

Things here go on just the same, drill, mimic attacks and route marches from morn till night until we are all dog tired. However I think the work suits me; it's a change for me to do any work. Even mother acknowledges I look better!

I may come down and see you on the first opportunity, mayn't I? I am reading "St. Ives"[22]; it's pretty good isn't it? Do you remember the "puritanical hens"?

Please forgive the emptiness of this letter; it isn't because I have nothing to say to you; but I can't say it well enough tonight. When I do tell you it will have to be in the finest way I can.

Please write to me soon, dear, and let me know how much better you are. I do miss you now and the quotation on Rossetti's picture applies with double force.

Goodbye dear girl,

Jack

Head Quarters,
9,Tufton Street,
Westminster S.W.
Monday night.

---

[22]'St. Ives: Being The Adventures of a French Prisoner in England' by Robert Louis Stevenson. "Puritan hens" are mentioned in the text.

35

My dear,

Thank you very much for R.L.S., your good wishes and your letter. When you are away I would rather be with Robert Louis than anyone. That you should send me something of his on my birthday is one of the things I would most have happened. There could not be a finer token of the friendship and comradeship that have been between us and the love there is now. May, from the first we have trusted one another completely, and I am sure that is what has puzzled those who could not understand our relations. To some extent the "comet gas" has been between us. It has made everything clear and so there are no sordid episodes we would forget. You have made the last two years unforgettable to me and real pessimism impossible. Life cannot be vain with such comradeship as ours has been. Nothing in my life has appealed to me more than the thought that you trust me completely. That, I think, would take me through anything and keep me straight if everything else failed. My dear, I can love you for yourself, not as fulfilling some preconceived ideal but us making one.

I shall be able to come down to Horsham, and quite soon, I hope. Then we will have a perfect day. There was no reason why I should be dropped upon for depot duty; it was pure chance as directed by the Colonel.

It is splendid to hear you are really better. The country is essential to you and one day you must go to live in it. Then you will have your garden. You must not work too hard at knitting; it will not do for you to worry about finishing it so much, although I want the socks. I will not be a taskmaster!

Please thank Grace very much for her note and good wishes. I have more friends than I deserve.

My dear, you will forgive this letter; I feel that I must write it and tell you how much you mean to me and how much I owe you. Tonight I can tell you that I love you without feeling it to be the presumption it once would have been.

Goodbye dear,

Jack

Head Quarters,
Westminster S.W.
Thursday evening

My dear,

Thanks so much for the socks. They fit splendidly and I have no criticism to make on them other than the most favourable. I am not speaking now as a high court official. My dear girl, you make a mistake in assigning me the office you do. In reality I am a soothsayer by trade. The hag-clerk and others who have told you the truth will support my assertion.

I should like to come and see you on Saturday. I can leave Victoria by the 8.55 train and get to Horsham at 9.55, the train starting a hour earlier gets to Horsham only 12 minutes before this one, and besides, I cannot very well leave till Capt. Monro turns up in the morning, generally a few minutes past 8. He is staying in the afternoon and evening for me so I am afraid I must be back by eight at the latest. Still, from 10 in the morning will be a gloriously long day for us to be together in the real

37

country; the worst of it is that it will go so quickly, spent with you, dear.

The Colonel told me this morning that I should probably want a change so I hope to go on to Epsom later.

I shall have lots to tell you on Saturday and you lots to show me. Until then I drink to "the Day", the most perfect we've yet had together.

Goodbye dear,

Jack

Head Quarters,
9, Tufton Street,
Westminster S.W.

My dear,

I hope you weren't too tired before you got home last night, and had company. I was back in London before I knew it and had not finished reading the second Punch[23]. What a splendid day it was, dear! but so short. After "Final" we must have another day out together. It will be winter almost then and we have never been in the country together when the leaves have fallen, and the bare woods grow dark purple in the grey afternoons. Besides, we must see the round of the seasons where they can only be seen, in the country. As Hardy sees the world go round,

---

[23]Punch was a British weekly magazine of humour and satire

standing on a hill and watching the stars move over the sky, so we can see ourselves whirled through time and yet feel stable.

Later on, when we are much older the feeling of stability may weaken, but now it is possible; chiefly, I suppose, because we are together. Hardy watched alone and saw the hideous vastness of the sky, its emptiness, inhumanity and crushing power. He felt these things alone and so felt life itself to be awful, too unyielding for one soul to bear. May, the only thing that makes the world habitable is companionship. Without it the beauty of Nature is only a screen to hide its cruelty; and alone one can see the wolf's eyes behind it.

My dear, the one great dread of my life is loneliness; I have known what it is and it is not an imaginary fear. You have saved me from that and tonight I look back on what might have been and shudder.

The finest thing in the "Four Men"[24] is what Greybeard says on friendship. May, while I have the quintessence of friendship, which is the greatest thing in the world, I don't envy the world in anything.

I have had a sort of millstone round my neck all day today in the shape of a motor lorry. It takes stores down to Epsom and breaks down at convenient moments (for the driver). This means incessant phoning and counter-phoning and I have just sent it home as hopeless, much to the driver's delight. "He ain't

---

[24]This reference is obscure – it may refer to 'Four Men in a Cave' by Stephen Crane (1871-1900)

got no headlights and a nuts worked orf". What he really means is that he's had enough work today. "But it ain't safe guv'ner and I might get killed a'driving that there thing", to me urging a third journey. I will not have murder on my soul so the Camp gets no more stores today, and the transport officer swears over the telephone.

This morning a major dropped in and scared me, but he was quite tame and even pleasant.

For the rest, I have had nothing to do but read tactics and write this long epistle to you. It shall not occur too often so please forgive it.

Have you heard from Grace yet? And you are not worrying too much over that affair? Until "Final", you know dear, you must only work and keep well, especially the second.

Please write to me when you can, but only when you can well afford the time. You must not stay in to write.

There is only one more week of country for you and it must be made the best of.

And so to bed.

> Goodnight dear girl,
>
> Jack

Head Quarters,
9, Tufton Street,
Westminster S.W.

Dear May,

The very worst happened last night. About half past nine, just as I had finished packing, the doctor hauled me up for a medical exam and failed me on account of my heart. So I'm on depot duty after all with no chance of seeing Malta yet awhile. However I still cherish hope of going later. I mean to see a private doctor and find out what is really wrong with my heart and whether it can be cured or at least put fairly right. You see I was very low last night after the three days rush and whatever the trouble it was accentuated. I'll nurse myself up just before I see the doctor next time and then perhaps I can scramble through. Then let's hope it will be away to the Tideless Sea[25].

I must stay here tonight and as you go to Sussex tomorrow I shall not see you till you come back. Anyhow come back well and ready for Sussex.

I started my real duties today and am just going to look after some thirty men. Tomorrow parades and drill start. Later on we are going into Camp, perhaps Aldershot, and to the ranges for shooting practice. I think we go to Purfleet. That will be fair, but curse our Scotch doctor!

    Goodbye dear,

    Jack

Head Quarters,
9, Tufton Street,

---

[25]The Mediterranean

Westminster S.W.
Saturday morning

My dear,

I have just got your letter. Of course I shall write to you as often as I can, and you know I should have written before if I could have got to know your address before.

It seems, after all, that I shall not go to Epsom. I am to be left in charge of the depot, for a time at least. Having once got a commission my luck seems to have drained away. Anyway I have started reading tactics and various military books; it seems I shall have a chance of mixing Old English and the like with these. This is very nice in a way but field work would be a hundred times better. Perhaps the gods will grant me that later.

Thank you very much for your good wishes; although it's not your birthday I may return them, for you are in Sussex. I'm glad you're having a time worthy of the noble country. Carry on!

Yours,

Jack

Head Quarters,
9, Tufton Street,
Westminster S.W.

Dear May,

I wasn't here last night in time to get your letter so I came on and just missed you. In fact I met Hugh coming back from the trams. It's fine for you to go to Highgate for a week, it will really do both you and your work good. Then you will get real benefit since you can do just as you like, you know restraint worries and upsets you like it did at the Hostel. Here there's nothing but work. Today I was up at five, drilling and marching men at quarter to six and again at half past eight. I had just ten minutes for breakfast and twenty for dinner and so went on till six. I am earning my 5/3 don't you think?

The Captain assures me that I shall go abroad right enough so I am considerably bucked. I get continually bad-tempered in thinking about that wretched Scotch doctor and his theories about hearts. What a thing it would be aboard ship in the Mediterranean now just in sight of Malta, with a further chance of going to France! The lucky beggars!

I'm off duty tomorrow evening, dear, so could you meet me in Deans Yard[26] say at 6.30? I do want to see and talk to you again. However don't put anything else off for it.

I have nothing more I will tell you till I see you.

Goodbye, Good Luck, dear,

Jack

P.S. Don't trouble to let me know, I will be there at 6.30. If you can't come tomorrow, I shall be off duty on Friday and can meet you at the same time.

---

[26]A private, secluded square adjacent to Westminster Abbey

Head Quarters,
9, Tufton Street,
Westminster S.W.

Dear May,

I have looked up the list of amusements tonight for tomorrow night. There doesn't seem to be much on at the Music Halls. However, here is a list of the likely Variety entertainments-;

Alhambra "Not Likely" Varieties 8.30

Revue 9.00

Palace "The Passing Show" 8.0

Revue 8.55

New Middlesex "Faust" 7.30

Scala Kinecolor 8.0

Among the theatres are:-

Kingsway "The Great Adventure" 8.20

Lyric "The Chocolate Soldier" 8.15

Prince of Wales "When Knights Were Bold" 8.45

Royalty "My Lady's Dress" 8.30

All mean you must arrange to be out late, I should like to be in if possible at 11.30; you see I couldn't stroll in at 12 or past and wake everybody up, and I couldn't very well get home at something like 1 o'clock to be up the next morning at 5.0. Perhaps you can advise a way and means. Any rate we will go somewhere amusing and you shall not be hustled about as you were last evening.

I found my way home quite well last night and slept after all at Headquarters. It was too late to get to East Ham.

Please excuse this note and overlook illegibility and mistakes. I am very sleepy after an all day parade, but I shall not be so tomorrow night with you beside me.

Goodnight dear,

Jack

296, Katherine Road,
Forest Gate, E.
Sunday.

My dear May,

 You see I am writing from home so you may get a letter before you leave Highgate in exchange for one you may have sent me. You were not too late on Friday night? I got in about 12 o'clock, and made a bed of a pile of blankets whereon I slept the sleep of the just.

Do you know the "Passing Show" has left no impressions on my mind except one of its hollowness and another of its underlying coarseness. Infidelity and the meanness and selfishness of it and underlying filth are not funny. To laugh at them seems to me like finding amusement in a loathsome sore wrapped in coloured bandages. The brilliance of colour and sparkle only serve to intensify the feeling of disgust when I look back on it.

My dear, I am still wearing my uniform and have not yet

exchanged it for cassock and bands so please excuse this preaching. I am really glad we went; it was worth the experience, but I don't want to go again.

Thank you so much for writing to Mother. She was pleased and asked me to tell you she will be in next Thursday afternoon if you care to come and see her.

You know there's really nothing to write to you about, and if there were, my brain as usual of late, is too dull to put it into writing. I seem to be perpetually in a doze nowadays. I want to talk to you; writing seems poor when I can do that, so until Tuesday evening.

Goodbye, dear,

Jack

Head Quarters,
9, Tufton Street,
Westminster S.W.

My dear,

I was so glad to hear this morning that Norman was better and your Father too. I shall not be able to come down tonight as I have to take a party down to Epsom this evening and not this afternoon as I thought. But I have arranged with Captain Munro to get off tomorrow afternoon about 4 o'clock and so shall be down before tea. I do want to see you again so much. Till then,

Goodbye dear,

Jack

Head Quarters,
9, Tufton Street,
Westminster S.W.
Friday morning.

My dear,

Thank you very much for your letter; I was very glad to get it.
Unless you hear to the contrary I will come to see you on
Monday evening. Let me know if that is not convenient. I will
bring 'Sussex' along with me so that we can look at it together. I
could not resist the temptation of glancing through some of the
illustrations and I think you will like them. I took a third party
of men down to Epsom last night and now we have only sixty
men left here. They, like the baby's Mellin's Food[27], will soon be
"all gone". On the march this morning I was talking with an old
colour-sergeant who remembers the muzzle-loading cannon
and used to carry a bag of spikes with him to spike the guns if
they were in danger of capture. Just as they used to at Waterloo!

I went to King's yesterday lunch hour and found the place
deserted. A third of the men have joined the ranks or got
commissions and of the rest about three quarters have joined
the O.T.C. I heard that Shawyer has got to the firing line. Isn't he
lucky to have got out so soon? But there really seems a chance
of our going to France in three months or so, perhaps before;

---

[27]The production of Mellin's Food for Infants was carried on for some years,
about 1900–10, in a large factory in Redclyffe Road less than a mile from
Jack and May's London homes. "Soon be all gone" presumably refers to an
advertising slogan.

and even if it is only to guard communications, it will not be bad.

Yes, dear, I understand about "unbelievable" in as far that I know it is not because you can't or don't want to tell me, I am content to wait the time. Perhaps when the time comes when you promised to tell me some things you will be able to tell me all.

You are right, May, Saturday was incomplete; but you will let me complete it on Monday?

    Goodbye dear,

    Jack

 P.S. No, we will not pick a cold day for the country, but one of those bright clear days when walking is a perfect joy and the sun too bright for chilliness.

296,Katherine Road,
Forest Gate.E.
Sunday afternoon.

My dear,

Thanks very much for your postcard; and you had a good journey down? What a rush Friday must have been; and no light porter for your bag! I would not call the morning you went because you were not to be hindered and for a less prosaic reason. Still, it was rotten you should have gone off by yourself, and I was free all day, too.

The prospect of training is good, isn't it? Barker seems to think there will be no trouble. With a good second and training you will be in the clouds. But you have drawn your hair back? B.A.'s don't need to, really, you know; it's only German governesses who do it, and you'll never make a good imitation of a Fraulein, you scamp.

It's no good my trying to write anything but the most stodgy letter; it's a wet Sunday afternoon and I've had my dinner. For dullness what more could you want? Whatever you say in your letter that's to come, I'm sure your Maths. lessons went off alright. I never made a more certain prophecy than that about your teaching; and when I said the children's luck was in I declared a truth worthy of my office. Wisdom cometh ahead and you must regard it. No, I'm not a "bombastic young man".

We haven't started business up at Headquarters yet, but I hope we shall next week. Meanwhile, I come home as usual and find the evenings some ten hours long.

I can't write any more this afternoon, dear, things are too dull, and my brain is also. I must have your letter to sharpen it.

By the way, Mother sends congratulations to you and confirms my statement that the khaki socks fit splendidly.

Good luck and goodbye dear girl,

Jack

296, Katherine Road,
Forest Gate E.
Monday evening.

Dear May,

I got your letter this evening after spending the afternoon, in desperation, with Lewis at the Palladium. Of course the show was no good, slightly more childish and certainly more stupid than the "Palace".

It has just dawned on me that you have a Sunday delivery in a country town. I thought that it would make no difference whether I wrote on Saturday or Sunday and that you could not get a letter before Monday. Please forgive my muddleheadedness. I am sorry I could not see you off; I have consistently done the wrong thing this last day or two, but again, please forgive me.

I say, how busy you'll be; it'll be a strain to start with, but I'm sure you'll be master quite easily and soon especially as the boys are not small. Not having so much Geography will save you some work.

I'm surprised the country is so flat, but it'll be interesting and besides, when we next go into Essex together I shan't have to point out every hill. Still, Sherwood is near, isn't it? And the Midland woods are fine; you'll have Epping magnified and such colours, too, in the bare woods, a background for "Christabel". It's good that your window looks on to the castle and the work in the old classroom will be improved by its age. Even Maths. will be romantic and you'll look splendid, gowned, with dark wood and old walls for a background. While the study, my-one-time room, will be no longer envied. By the way, let me know, please, the books you want; I've almost lost the art of book-buying. It's splendid having the afternoons free; and you won't

50

find the Midlands "sodden and unkind". Instead they'll be another place on our tour programme, along with Cornwall, Suffolk, Sussex, Whitby etc, etc.

What do you think, Kings' have got two firsts in English (and Pink is top of the University) among the men, and two for the girls. It's good for us isn't it? I saw Gladys Philpots' card - what happened among the others?

I remembered my "guidebook" appointment on Friday and I think Hugh was interested. We hadn't time to do the Chapels, besides a verger took people round. We are going one day this week when they are open.

Garland and I have started fencing and semaphore and do fill in some of the time, but it hangs heavy. I do want some real work.

Your journey with the soldiers was good; you stuck to it well and the other woman <u>was</u> a coward to leave you to it alone.

Goodbye dear, and please forgive my letter being behind; it wasn't from indifference or lack of thought, and success to your adventure!

     Jack

296, Katherine Road,
Forest Gate E.
Sunday afternoon.

My dear,

How are you getting on, and are you really better? I heard you had a touch of the 'flu; you should let me know. Please write to me soon about your doings in Nottingham. My name appeared in Friday's Gazette as transferred to the Territorial Reserve, so you see I am more or less stranded. They don't seem to have taken any notice of my application for the transfer to be cancelled. Isn't it cussed of them?

Anyhow, I'm spending tomorrow trying to get the transfer, but I am not very sanguine of the result. If I succeed I expect it means waiting at home for three weeks or so and I'm at present wondering what I'm to do for that time. I think of applying to the "Cedars" (the headquarters in West Ham Park[28], you know) for a temporary job. In case I can't get the transfer cancelled I shall have to apply to the War Office to get another transfer to a Territorial Unit. This would probably take a month to go through; but I think I should get something.

Naturally, I was disappointed since I was just going to start real work in the new Battalion and had the prospect of a rise in pay and a promotion. Still, the Reserve gets some pay, but how much I don't know. You see I am a miser still. However, my luck may change with the New Year. Meanwhile I think about starting Icelandic, so I can teach you and be a teacher too! It will be a good advertisement later in applying for a post. "Coached a post-graduate in Icelandic and Scandinavian Antiquities".

Mother has been to Nottingham; she says the country is very pretty a little way out and that all she remembers of the town are the red tiled roof tops. I'm just reading one of Gissing's; I've not got far enough yet to know whether I like him. I see there's

---

[28]A park very close to Jack and May's homes, where the T.A. can still be found.

an edition of his "Private Papers of Henry Rycroft"[29]. I must send it to you. Lewis says it's very good; and he's really a good judge of literature, you know.

Have you done any correspondence coaching in Latin yet? How does <u>setting</u> exam papers suit? My dear, please write and tell me about yourself soon; East Ham is not particularly interesting now and I do want someone to talk to me.

Jack

296, Katherine Road,
Forest Gate E.
Saturday.

My dear,

I got your testimonial typed this morning and send you the copies. I hope you won't need a place - the East Ham people should give you the grant alright. Still, of course you must apply. There's absolutely nothing happens here and no news. What a good testimonial Hilton has written you, and so true! I am glad when you get things like that and it makes me so proud.

I am still waiting a reply from the Territorial Association and some work. With luck both should come soon.

Goodbye dear girl,

Jack

---

[29]'The Private Papers of Henry Rycroft' by George Gissing Archibald Constable (1907)

296, Katherine Road,
Forest Gate,E.
Monday evening.

My dear,

You are really better? You must let the teaching go hang rather than get ill.

The book of parodies is for an irreverent mood. The greatness of the originals must be forgotten for the moment and only the grotesque imitations of the mimicry remains to laugh at. And some of them are jolly good criticism too.

I have been more successful today than I hoped. It seems that I shall belong to the 2nd. Battalion though on the reserve and receive the pay (except for the 1/9 allowance). I saw the Colonel this morning and he wants me to apply once more to the War Office for transfer to Kitchener's Army and if that fails he says there will be no difficulty in getting back into the Territorials again. He will not believe that the War Office officials have assured me three times that this transfer is impossible; but a letter from them will convince him. I expect this in a few days and then I think things will be just as they were again. Also I retain my seniority while on the Reserve and so I hope to lose nothing by this silly business. Still, it has been very worrying and it gave me the 'blues' during the weekend.

Your note dispelled them this morning since you say you are better. Please forgive the scrawl as I write under difficulties.

Yours,

Jack

296, Katherine Road,
Forest Gate E.
Wednesday morning.

My dear, dear girl,

Thank you so much for your letter. It is good to hear you are getting over the 'flu; but you must be careful of your throat so that you come back better than when you went.

You must believe me, dear, there is no chance at all of my being miserable for more than a very few hours while I have you as a comrade and your confidence and love. It will never be hard work for you to make me happy; the friendship and comradeship that have been between us and the love that now is, form, as I've told you before, May, the most perfect thing in my life. My love, with such perfection to look back upon and look forward to, how can I be wretched for any time? Our lives have steadily come closer and closer until now they have started to run parallel.

In you I have the two most precious things in life; an ideal to live by and a trust which will protect me from any calamity life may bring. I cannot express to you this morning the feeling of absolute triumph in me. That, my dear heart, shall be left until we meet again, when it will be so easy. This morning I can look into the future with no misgiving. May, with such faith in each other as we have, living, we need fear no fate and years will but make us old lovers.

My affairs seem to get more and more complicated. I saw a staff major at the War Office the day before yesterday who recommended me to ask the Colonel to cancel my transfer to

55

the Reserve. Yesterday, before I had done so, he wrote me a private note advising me to try room MT3 at the War Office, to see whether they would give me a temporary commission in the Regulars, before I asked the Colonel to cancel the transfer. Wasn't it good of him? Especially since I only saw him for about three minutes. However, MT3 would not give me a Regular commission and a captain there told me that the only way to get one was to resign my Territorial Commission and apply for another in Kitchener's. But he strongly recommended me not to do this. Moreover, I can't resign during wartime. It is for this reason, you see, I can't join as a private.

I next 'phoned up the Colonel to ask him to cancel. I told him what the War Office had said; he replied it was my own affair. When I asked him to cancel he said he certainly would not. "In fact" he said "I don't care what you do as long as you don't come down here" I assured him I should never do that and rang off. Next, I went to the Territorial Association (a sub-committee of the War Office to look after the City of London Territorials). I stated my case to them and asked what I should do. The captain there advised me to apply to my Colonel for restoration to the strength in writing, and if he refused to send in a statement in full of my case to them and they would move in the matter.

So you see I have the Association behind me, so that if the Colonel refuses to consider my application, as I expect he will, there will be a stand up row and with the help of the Association I stand a fair chance of winning. This is getting quite exciting for me, dull enough as it must sound to you. I have given up the attempt to get into the Regulars since I've seen five separate Staff Officers each of whom has assured me it is impossible.

You know you have been not nearly careful enough of yourself, continuing teaching as you have with 'flu and a bad throat; you must reform and repent and alter your ways and walk in the paths of carefulness. I'm glad you found some country and I hope you'll find Sherwood before you come back. You will if anyone can, you dryad. How fine for you to go out to see Hilton's friends like that. These sort of outings will help to stop you feeling lonely and dull.

Please do not think of me as having a cold; mine has been but an apology for one, and even now has left scarce a wrack behind. You must have been hard at work on exam papers; do you believe setting them is worse than suffering them to be set upon one? And you'll write and tell me how your Speech-day went off and leave me to picture how splendid you looked; as you did on one other similar occasion.

Goodbye my love,

Jack

296, Katherine Road,
Forest Gate E.
Thursday evening.

Dear girl,

By this time your cold should be well and your throat too. I hope you have been careful enough to bring this about. You are answerable to me too, you know. My affairs are progressing; as I expected the Colonel refused to apply for my restoration to the strength so I have prepared a written statement of my case (3 pages of typewriting) and forwarded it to the Territorial Association. I now await results.

Garland is almost as enthusiastic as I am in this hustle with the C.O. He, too, has suffered! But I am very proud of my statement; it is most legal and in type it looks most impressive!

And do IVB keep on their good behaviour or have they required more correction? I should just think you can talk to nearly all of them. You said they weren't brilliant, but, my dear, they have some intelligence.

I have ordered an Icelandic Primer to occupy my time during this lull in the storm, but believe me, I am not desperate and I feel cheerful, even excited at the prospect of something happening soon. If I can't get back into the Territorials I'm going to try to get my commission cancelled and apply for another in Kitchener's Army, and if that fails there's the ranks. Out of so many opportunities I'm sure one will be a success.

I went out to tea with Garland last night, and do you know I actually got enthusiastic over Warner's "Albion's England"[30]. I wonder if that egg will ever be hatched! There is nothing more to tell you, but tomorrow or Saturday you shall have something better than a letter.

Goodbye, dear heart,

Jack

---

[30] A long poem in fourteen-syllabled verse by William Warner (1586).

There are only twelve more days before I see you again now; you must not doubt I'm really bucked.

296, Katherine Road,
Forest Gate E.
Friday evening

My dear,

I've nothing to write to you about and no excuse even; but now I can come and see you without an excuse, (I don't even have to bring "English Review"). I'll write to you with no more reason than because I want to. By the way, I bought the "English Review" to send you, but there was so little in it I would not.

(I lost my laugh yesterday, for College closed on Wednesday and accordingly Lewis had gone North.) I went on to Headquarters yesterday and learned that the 1st. Batt. is leaving for Malta on Tuesday; I am fated evidently not to go there; and so is Garland, he is left in charge of fifty men at Epsom. Do you wonder he was bad-tempered over the phone? The afternoon I spent in a like bad temper, but recovered in the evening and the reason for this later cheerfulness you know.

This morning I (please forgive all these I's) went to the Association to see whether Captain Harvey had forgotten me. He had not! He said that I should be absorbed into one of the Reserve Batts. now forming, not necessarily the 2nd. and that he would write and let me know which. He thought I should know in ten days or a fortnight. So at last I'm in sight of some work. The battalions now at Malta are going to France. Were I only there! But for evermore will I pity the unemployed.

I have just finished reading Kipling's "Wee Willie Winkie" - such splendid stories. Have you read it? If not you must. The worst of it was everybody therein was hard at work, so I envied my neighbour the whole time I was reading. One other book - Swift's "Journal to Stella"; it's jolly interesting, you feel you know Swift after reading it, and what an extraordinary man! He must have absolutely fascinated and dominated Stella, but I doubt whether he loved her or she him. He always writes to a pupil or daughter and never to a woman comrade.

I am now sitting in my little room and I do want to change the pictures. If I did I believe I should hear you knock at the door - the last month has seemed just like a year ago, only I have not seen you. But it is a thousand times better and there's only a weekend between us.

After reading Swift I blessed the 20th Century. He had to wait weeks and weeks to hear from Ireland and you are only a day away. Why, dear, you are but across the road. Comrade and college chum, we have another and a marvellous advantage. You have a third title added to these now, my love, to set them aflame; these three make our "Triumph of Life"[31]! You must not fear the jealous Gods; these things exist in our lives and nothing Fate can do can make them as though they had never been. Together we can go on and fear not.

Here end the meditations, not of Aurelius[32], but of one seeking

---

[31]A reference to Shelley's last poem?

[32]Roman Emperor Marcus Aurelius wrote his 'Meditations' during the 1st Century A.D.

to live up to a higher title.

Amantis[33]

296, Katherine Road,
Forest Gate E.
Monday evening.

My dear,

Mother got your letter this morning and thanks you very much for it. Of course I read it and I was jolly pleased to hear about the £12 cheque. You heiress! And how does marking suit? Guthketch used to declare that he'd rather sit for exams than mark the results of one. But you don't think so; finals are not long enough over yet. Are you really almost well now? You must come home <u>quite</u> well, you know, dear.

On Saturday Garland had orders to proceed to Epsom with the fifty new recruits to take charge of the Camp left vacant by the 1st. Reserve Batt. going into billets at Tunbridge Wells. Won't he have a splendid time down there in sole charge, with only fifty to look after? I think about going down to see him for a couple of days this week if the weather is at all fine. I fancy Tunbridge billets explain the Colonel's rotten temper these days.

Icelandic is actually started and I did a bit of painting this morning, but I don't think this sort of thing will last very long, for I heard this afternoon that Captain Harvey (the man I saw at

---

[33]Latin, meaning lover, and probably refers to *Confession Amantist*, a 14th century Middle English poem by John Gower.

the Association) is solely responsible for the officers of the new Reserve Batt., and he seemed quite willing to get me into that when I saw him the other day.

My dear, I do want you back home again to be with me and fill East Ham. It's been empty since you went away. But you are having a good time now and making a splendid teacher; the boys must just love you (despite exams and such silliness) and what more proof do you want? Your prospects are too good for you to go to East Dereham, but I like to fancy you there, right in East Anglia and the flats. I could come and see you just once, couldn't I? It would be so splendid to be with you there, among the farms with the thatched and tiled houses and barns. All this is a dream, with you as a teacher at East Dereham; but with we two as wanderers in the highways and byways of East Anglia or Sussex, that is more than a dream, sweet heart, that is an expectation.

So, goodbye my love,

Jack

296, Katherine Road,
Forest Gate E.
Thursday.

My dear,

Of course I will meet you and please let me know what time your train comes and to what station. It will be splendid to see you again and I shall have to use a deal of self control not to be at the station an hour or so too early.

You must be working hard, and marking Scripture! but I forgot, you are a Sunday School teacher. I am glad that you are really well and having a good time. I am sure of the latter from your letter. Here nothing, absolutely nothing, happens and I spend the days working at Icelandic and semaphore, reading and tactics. I am going up to London this morning to rake up Lewis and laugh.

There is nothing more to tell you, so

Goodbye dear girl,

Jack

Only four more days!

Christmas Eve.

My love,

 This to wish you Christmas happiness and the best the New Year can bring. Comrade, I have seen the Splendour of Life today; may this be yours and mine through the years.

Jack

296, Katherine Road,
Forest Gate, E.

My dear,

Following the custom of the house I too, am in bed with the 'flu

63

and so I can't come and see you tonight. I am so sorry, I wanted to talk to you badly. I hope I shall be able to come on Saturday afternoon.

I do hope I didn't pass the infection on to you on Wednesday. I had no idea 'flu was so catching.

Please excuse this fearful scrawl, writing in bed makes my bad hand ten times worser!

Goodbye,

Jack

3rd/2nd. City of London Royal Fusiliers
Tattenham Corner,
Epsom,
4/3/1915.

My dear,

Thank you so much for your letter and your painting. May, it is jolly good and the drawing too. Please go on and send me some more. One point, put more paint on and wetter. My scribble on the envelope was not an excuse but the truth and nothing but the truth. Today for example - I got up at 5.30 a.m. and walked 2½ miles to the riding school and had an hour's riding. By the way we use polo ponies, and a folded blanket for a saddle, our hands on our hips or behind our backs - no stirrups and no touching the reins. The horses walk, then trot and finally canter and gallop - this in the first lesson.

Of course the result is, on an average 3 tosses a lesson, but the turf is soft and our heads hard. But, my dear, it's splendid, you must learn one of these days. To proceed with the days routine - half an hour for breakfast - 9-12.30. drill on Epsom Downs. Then follows an hour for dinner and we go for a 2½ hours route march. Tea is graciously granted us. Officially we are then free, really work goes on, especially for Company Commanders and acting Company Commanders.

Last night I had to lecture the men on discipline, tonight I was member of a Court of enquiry and must take evidence of witnesses. Now the plates clatter for dinner which, by the way, counts as a parade and is over about 9 o'clock. After dinner there is correspondence to be answered - today 9 letters from the Adjutant and goodness knows who, await me. At 12 midnight one is allowed to go to bed. But the life here is splendid and I feel absolutely fit, my face is almost as red as my nose all over! But enough of myself - how are you and are you solemnly careful still? I hope so for the weekend approaches! You will be a Croesus or rather Croesa[34] with your teaching and coaching - you learned person. So Clem[35] is actually going and engaged - I wish him luck and please congratulate your sister for me.

I've got to know all sorts of interesting people and I shall have lots to tell you about them at the weekend. My dear, I am looking forward to it, I want you still as much as ever though

---

[34]Croesus was a legendarily wealthy king of Lydia from 560/561 BC until his defeat by the Persians in about 547 BC; Croesa is the feminine form of the name.

[35]Alfred Clements, who survived the war and later married May's sister Grace.

life is now as full as ever it can be.

The military postman is waiting for me so goodbye, dear heart,

> Jack

> Tattenham Corner,
> Epsom,
> Thursday.

Dear girl,

Thank you so much for your letter - but you must look after your cold; please get well by the weekend. My luck's in, I can get away this weekend again, so I hope to see you on Saturday afternoon, only you must let me know if you've arranged to go out, and please don't put anything off. May, I'm so pleased you got on well with mother on Monday. You two must be good friends.

Things here have settled down to routine - Felon gives the 2nds. an hour's squad drill before breakfast, another after breakfast and two in the afternoon. It's splendid exercise and jolly useful but real hard work and more than a little monotonous. However, we believe he goes next week so we can go on with horseriding again. My special duty now is filling in "crime sheets" and the number in this battalion is terrible. I think you could give the prisoners company drill.

The orderly has just come to say the postman is here - therefore a full stop.

> My dear, goodbye till Saturday,

Your own Jack

Tattenham Corner,
Epsom.
9/3/15

My dear,

How is your cold? Are you still careful? Are you taking things easily? My cross examination is done.

I caught a train on Sunday night at 9.40 and had company - it was quite good for guesswork. Filon is giving us Squad drill morning noon and night, and alas riding is off until his departure. But we hope they will go on soon. I thought things were going to be easier this week, but there's very little difference for now. My Captain (Towse is his name) has come back, the other sub. is gone to Chelsea for a fortnight and there you are.

By the way inoculation[36] is likely to begin this week so I may have a couple of days with you - who would not have inoculation? I can't write you anything like an interesting letter tonight, my brain seems to have stopped working and I have no pens, paper or envelopes.

Please send me some more paintings and a letter soon. My dear, I have been thinking about what is involved - May, it is as I've said before, the woman gives everything and the man next to

---

[36]Presumably against typhoid.

67

nothing. I can't bear to face the legal aspect - it's too horrible.

Comrade, I've nothing more to say. I must do my best and kiss your hand,

Goodbye,

Jack

Tattenham Corner,

Epsom.

My dear,

I have just got your letter, thank you so much. Together with it came the invitation to the Bedford "At Home"! I shall like coming with you to that. Last night 9 of us went in a car to Kingston "Empire", 8 miles away. The car went splendidly and we had a good time. It was so foggy coming home that we ran into the Bank several times but managed to get home safely. Really, believe me, it was the fog, nothing else. The C.O. badly wanted to come but couldn't.

Till tomorrow afternoon goodbye, dear heart,

Jack

P.S. Will you do me the honour of correcting two ridiculous spelling mistakes in my last letter? It was written in such a hurry - that's my only excuse - they have been worrying me ever since.[37]

---

[37] I find it interesting that Jack is clearly aware that May is saving his letters, and that they may be read by others. [Ed.]

Tattenham Corner,
Epsom.
Monday.

Dear girl,

You will be surprised as I was to hear that I am likely, as things stand now, to be off to France in a month or less. Garland told me the rumour that I and two others were to go out with the draft and one of the other subalterns has seen the telegram from the War Office, with my name as one of the three.

Of course everything may and probably will be altered again but the chance is here and things begin to be exciting.

I should be glad if you say nothing about this until I am more sure; These things are so uncertain and to go and then not go is as we know ridiculous.

I think I shall be able to come to town on Wednesday afternoon, Victoria about 1.34 I hope. However I will let you know definitely tomorrow.

Goodbye sweetheart,

Jack

Havre Packet,
11.30 p.m.
Wednesday night.

Dearest girl,

Here I am safely aboard the boat and ready to sail tomorrow

69

morning at 6 o'clock.

There was no trouble on arriving - the Embarkation Officer had our names and we were told to come this evening at 7 o'clock to see if our names were up for sailing tonight. They were. I've got a watch and fieldglasses and, above all £5[38]! I phoned up the manager of Cox's shipping agency here, a Mr. Chamberlain and asked about my business with Cox's bank. He was charming and at once offered to advance me £5 if I wrote a cheque - Lightbody gave me a blank one of his and there you are. By the way he invited me to his house and it was one of the most artistic I have been in lately - and he's got some splendid watercolours.

Everyone here from cabby to bank manager has treated me splendidly - they have been willing to (do) anything they could and tell us all they could.

The boat is fine and we travel 1st. class so I myself have a cabin.

My dear, we have had a good start. And, my love, this is probably the last unread letter I shall send you for a time. There is nothing left to be said after last night - oh, it is good my dear, to have that memory as the last till I come back.

Comrade, goodbye and au revoir. My love, good luck and fitness be yours till I come back. Sweetheart, I kiss you farewell.

Jack

---

[38]A considerable sum - an agricultural labourer's average weekly wage was less than £1 in 1914.

PART THREE
LETTERS FROM FRANCE

A Cafe,
Le Havres,
Thursday 5 o'clock.

My dear,

We got here about 12.30 today and after a jolly good lunch at Hotel M----[39] reported at Headquarters Base.

We go to Rouen tonight at 10 o'clock. Isn't it fine? I shall be able to see the cathedral. We had a simply splendid trip over - the sea was as calm as I have ever seen it and such a lovely green.

I got up this morning at 4.30 a.m.- before the boat started and so was on the boat deck when the sun rose and we made our way slowly down Southampton Water. May, it was splendid and I was in such good spirits and am awfully bucked now. I hope you are - you must excuse my talking about my doings at length, but I've been so interested today.

The people here are extraordinarily picturesque - blue and red trousered workmen with lovely wine-black velvet caps - the sort the French Quartier Latin are supposed to wear you know. The French "tommies" are pictures but so slovenly and unkempt - it's a treat to see the English "khakis" salute. Do you know there seem more British officers here than French, and Lightbody has met at least half a dozen fellows he knows.

We passed torpedo boats at Portsmouth and minesweepers.

---

[39]Hotel name censored.

Cruisers and one submarine going on the surface with a long trail of black smoke coming out of the back - it looked uncanny creeping along, like a long, black water snake.

My French is reviving quite well - I've been understood at once all day - by a taxi driver and workers and gendarmes. Don't forget I passed Inter in French! The wine here is fine, and at present a bottle between us.

I hope you got my telegram and note last night. We didn't get to bed until 2 and up at 4.30. It's a record! but I feel absolutely fit. In case you can't read the second paragraph of this letter - tomorrow I shall have a good time. Off tonight. Remember to write soon. Open any letters of mine. Understand I am quite well. Enjoy yourself as much as you can. Never overwork.

Oh, the cleverness of me!

My dear, try a letter to me addressed:

Lt.J.E.Richardson,

2nd. City of London Fusiliers

British Expeditionary Force

I can't give you any other address - only don't send anything important as it might go astray.

There is no more to say, but there will be quite soon.

Goodbye my dear,

Jack

Trenches
France.
11.30 a.m.

My dear girl,

I am writing this on Sunday morning with the British shells
passing over our heads, the German snipers occasionally
potting at us and aeroplanes sailing round and being followed
by white puffs from the smoke bombs fired by the anti-aircraft
guns. These white puffs look for all the world like pieces of
cotton wool.

I came into the trenches for four days last night about 6.30. We
marched along a railway line and then a road with just one or
two bullets whistling here and there but with no casualties. We
got safely into our breastwork and then followed a continual
fusillade from the German trenches 400 yards in front of us,
rifles, star bombs, and a search light. The result was nothing as
far as we were concerned. Still, it was a fine experience. I, with a
second lieutenant and two men were employed in building a
bombproof shelter with sandbags and boards, corrugated iron
etc.. The 2/Lieut.,to whom I am, of course junior, and I went on
duty of inspection of the whole line of the trenches from 1-3
p.m.and got to sleep at 3.30, to be roused at 5.0 this morning by
the "Stand To" when every man has to stand by his arms for an
hour. The Germans giving us quite a rifle bombardment as a
"reveille". They keep this up more or less all day and night. They
are just waking up again now. The rest of the morning we have
had nothing in particular to do except fire sometimes at the
Germans and keep our heads below the parapet. The British 4.7
guns have just started sending shells over us on to (one just

73

gone) the German lines. The last just burst over their trench. The Germans are using a trench mortar now, but not on us, on the trenches to our right.

The whole of the country here is desolate - the farms mere skeletons and the fields ploughed with earthworks. But, do you know May, I don't feel at all strange - almost exactly as if all the shots were blank and we were on field manoeuvres. I thought I should feel fearfully funky, but some how I don't. Besides it's such lovely weather today and the fellows here are jolly decent. I've even begun sketching the ruined houses etc. I must send you them when I manage to do some worth the transit.

We stay here in the trenches 4 days and then have 4 in billets. The latter are quite nice and we live in comparative luxury, although shells come quite close and knock corners off houses and break windows.(We just rushed into a dugout because an aeroplane coming over our trench was shelled and we're afraid of the shrapnel pieces - however none came).

What strikes me most is that the natives still stay with their homes and work in the fields even in the zone of fire. In the town the majority of the shops are open again, but it has a desolate look.

My love, I musn't tell you where I am, because my letters are not read and they trust me not to say anything censorable. But I can say we have Germans in a horseshoe round us and we are in one of the most advanced trenches of the Allied line. Swank!

My dear, this letter is very incoherent but I am writing things down as they occur to me. I am too lazy today to compose. Still, I hope you will find it interesting. And, comrade, do not be more anxious about me than you can help. There is really very little danger here and I am thoroughly enjoying myself. The business doesn't seem nearly so horrible now I am here. I'm in that frame of mind which is prepared to take the whole thing as a game, and a good one too. Anyhow I'm glad I'm not funky.

Comrade, please write to me soon and tell me all about yourself and how you are and what is happening. Now I am here I know nothing about the war!

This is a very bad drawing of my dugout. I will send you some better later.

> Au revoir darling,

> Jack

PS

Please don't let mother know how much I have told you as it would only worry her. I shall write her much shorter letters and leave out many things that may worry her though they will not worry you.

I don't know how I got the pages so muddled up but I think it makes sense if you read as they are numbered.

In May we will have a splendid time when I come back – that silver ring! This time not humorously, for I think we shall have had time by then, Comrade.

Trenches.
Tuesday March 23rd.1915
France.

Dearest girl,

Thank you so much for your letter, it was splendid, and do you know I had one from mother and one from Raphael all at the same time, i.e. yesterday evening about 5 o'clock.

I am so glad you and mother are getting on so well - it is good of you to look after her, she does want it. Still her letter was awfully cheery, and she says father is bucking up splendidly. It's the best news I could hear. Raphael's letter wasn't a bit cross - he has forgiven me and his letter is jolly charming.

Bravo dear over Miss H., - it's splendid! No more pessimism over teaching. I'm so bucked. Am I not a "vate"[40]? And isn't this a polite way of saying "I told you so?"

No, dear, please don't burn my letters to you because I shall certainly want them when I come back. Besides they will stand for so many special times later when we can hold them together. So please, please don't destroy them. Yes, you can burn Clem's - they mean nothing to me. I am so glad you have got the "Open Road" tho' I wish we could have bought it together. Do the illustrations come up to your standard, my critic? My comrade, it is the finest symbol of the bond between us that we could wish to have. I'm so glad you teased Ted - but you're right - you have to be careful for he is an impressionable

---

[40]Vate, Latin for a soothsayer or prophet.

76

youth!

You do understand why I can't let you know where I am, don't you? You see it's awfully decent of the C.O. and one musn't abuse the privilege. Did I tell in the last letter that there was snow on the ground when I got here? But the weather is splendid now - one can bask in the sun in the trenches - and it's really quite a lazy life I'm living now. Good luck to you in the exams - but you'll be alright and Miss H's report will take you anywhere.

Since I wrote to you on Sunday we have had two moves - first to some reserve trenches and then to a new advanced trench in the firing line. This one has some splendid "dugouts" where we slept warm and cosily enough last night. We had a "working party" too last night and in front of the trench parapet throwing up earth to strengthen it. It's rather exciting for the enemy send up rockets and star shells and light up the whole scene. Then we have to drop down and lie still until everything is dark again. However there isn't much real danger and it's jolly good exercise.

The moving from one trench to another is the worst job - the men have to be marched in single file through narrow, shallow communication trenches, sometimes for a mile or so. Hartington, my senior, goes in front and I in rear and we all creep all bent almost double until we get to the breastwork of the trench which we happen to be taking over. This is done, of course, just as it is dark, and the experience is eerie and exciting. But we have done well so far - no casualties altho' the bullets sing over us quite enough.

Barrington and I have been engaged this morning in making a well, and with an old biscuit tin and broken tiles we have been able to get quite clear water.

Just behind the trench is a row of four cottages ruined by shellfire and riflehail - the roof is nearly all off and the walls are riddled with holes. The remnants of furniture and bedding along with old clothes and pictures are littered about. I was there this morning collecting tiles to make our filter and picked up the small Virgin Mary medallion which I am sending. I've got a German shell case which didn't burst and I shall send it home if I can, tho' it's rather weighty. I'm enclosing a little drawing I made yesterday of a partially ruined house at the back of the trenches - just behind it is our field dressing station and a battery which sends shells over us on to the German lines - you hear a bang and then singing as they go over and finally the crash as the shrapnel bursts. It needs a day to get used to this but after that you don't notice them.

We expect to go out of the trenches tomorrow night and then we will have 3 days rest and luxury in the town and I must see about getting various equipment. Do you know, Burberry's have an agency here - so we can get almost anything.

I will try to write you another rigmarole tomorrow, but never get worried if a letter doesn't come as one never knows what there is to be done and whether there will be time to write.

Au revoir, sweetheart,

Jack

P.S. Please thank your people for their kind wishes and tell Norman I'll write to him soon. I'm glad you've got him a badge.

78

He can have two regiments under his command now.

P.S. By the way it's quite true what you hear about the German prisoners - they are only too glad to be taken. A few days ago some 70 were taken to Havre under one English guard and he went to sleep and left his rifle by his side!

P.S. My dear, will you send me a paper now and again as we have no news here. But, remember, it must not take the place of your letters, dear heart.

Trenches
March 24th.1915.
Wed. afternoon.

My dear,

We've had rain and rain since early yesterday evening and we really are pictures to behold. The trenches are some 4 or 5 inches deep in mud, you can't distinguish the shape of our boots for the mud round them and my puttees are caked in it up to the knees.

Alas, for my new jacket, it is also mud all over, and my cap is like a pancake in shape and peasoup in colour - I look like a fair specimen of a tramp. I am writing this under a waterproof sheet rigged up as a tent, with one puttee off and one on, no cap and a goat skin jacket. Anyhow I've just had a wash! Things are very quiet today - they haven't even shelled us, and the snipers are very quiet.

I think the rain has dulled their spirits also. We go out of the trenches tonight for 4 days "rest". This usually consists of digging trenches for other companies, carrying wood and sandbags up to the firing line and route marches. On the whole I think the men prefer the trenches. But the fellows are jolly good. Of course they grumble, but it soothes them and they're really in the best of spirits and they work like Trojans to the admiration of the Regulars.

Just before I came they dug trenches for the North Staffords when the latter had advanced some 300 yards. They were under fierce fire all the time but were covered by the fire of the Staffs.. They dug to such purpose that the trenches we now occupy were the result and they are some of the most advanced and nearest Berlin! An account of the affair was in the papers.

I've got a timefuse, the nosepiece, of a German shell which I'm sending home if I can. It's quite undamaged and shows the scale by which the bursting of the shell is regulated.

By the way, I had quite a funny sleep-walking experience the night before last. It appears I got up and walked out of the back of the trench (they were reserve and so not near the enemy) and remarked to the sentry -- "Monsieur, òu peut-on trouver Monsieur Harrington, s'il vous plait?"[41] I remembered asking the question in the morning but of whom and when I didn't know until the sentry told me. He thought I'd had a double dose of rum, but I'm sure it wasn't that. Harrington found me before that upside down in bed. But really I don't think it was the rum!

I shall be jolly glad to get back to town tonight, chiefly because we can have a warm bath and get clean. Besides it will be a

---

[41]"Where might I find Mr Harrington please sir?"

great thing to have a good sleep and in a bed too. I don't think the above gives away any official secrets; It'll do the Germans no good to know we have the luxury of a town every now and then!

How are the exams going? Really going into Final on the first day seems much worse than going into the trenches for the first time seemed the other day. However none of us will be sorry to see the end of the war - this life is jolly interesting and exciting for a time, but after a few months I should think it becomes well nigh unbearable and monotonous. Anyhow I'm awfully bucked to be here and I think my three days between training camp and firing line is something of a record.

My dear, it's time this yarn ended; but I should like to see you this evening - what a gossip we could have! However I shouldn't be surprised if 6 months finished the war and then some will have to be spent in occupation perhaps, though they might send us home and use other troops for that. Still leave is a possibility and I'm only a day's journey from you. It's worth dreaming of, sweetheart!

Goodbye, dear one. I've got a vision of the time that's waiting for we two as a background to the wonderful life I'm having now. And, comrade, you at home are the most wonderful of all. We have nothing to put up with here as compared with you. You're bricks!

Your own,

Jack

Billets.
Thursday.
My dear,

I spent a lovely, lazy day in town after the trenches; but it has been weird enough and wonderfully interesting. This morning Lightbody and I went shopping and aired our "pigeon" French with quite good success. A cigarette lighter, an electric torch, some flares, some wine, chocolate and dates - not a bad mixture. About 4 this afternoon we found a sort of cafe where one could get "5 o'clock tea" as well as wine.

We sat here for some time until there was only one officer left (when we first came, the place was full of them). He began to play the piano and he played splendidly too, and then he whistled, accompanying the piano and finally sung. He told us he was once principal baritone in Carl Rosa and then joined the Army with a commission in the Artillery. He was stationed at a place nearby and had had one week's rest since the war began, and this was the first time he had seen a piano for seven months.

Every day, he told us, he had to go to his observation tower along a road swept by bullets and he escaped death daily. Time and time again officers who went with had been killed or badly wounded, but he still remained and was going back to it tomorrow. "But this observation work," he said "was the finest of all, and the Artillery the finest regiment of the Army."

And then he played some more and sang Italian songs. You can just imagine what it was like - the cafe was panelled in dark oak, lit by oil lamps, shaded, with two other officers and ourselves at a table and the artillery man playing and singing at the piano. One of the other two had been out since the war began and had been through Mons and the Aisne without more than a flesh wound. And this was his birthday and he was celebrating it. There was one, who looked about 19 or 20, a 2/Lieut. in a Scotch regiment who had been through it all. He and one other were all that were left of the officers of his battalion. And we sat and drank tea and later wine and listened while they talked.

But the look in their eyes, May, it meant ten years of life for them, I'm sure. At 8 o'clock we left and we had to help the one whose birthday it was home. He had celebrated it too well - but he was quiet - it only made him talk of the last 7 months and that wasn't boisterous chatter.

And the streets here are ghostly enough at night. There are no civilians allowed out of their houses after 8 o'clock and no lights are allowed either in the streets or windows. Everything is closed down. You go down old-fashioned cobbled streets, and tonight they were white in the moonlight, with only a sentry here and there with fixed bayonet and sometimes a transport limber passing. Here and there is a house with great holes in the walls or roof, where a German shell has landed; and the Town Hall clock looks down on you with half it's face blown away. It is, at night, absolutely a town of the dead - a city of dreadful night and the guns boom all the time.

We are now in a billet in a little poor house of an old French workman and his wife. They sleep in the cellar, we have the attic upstairs. I talked a long time tonight with the old lady - she told me about her three sons at the war and showed me their letters. Of course she is awfully proud of them - one is with a mitrailleuse[42], two are in the artillery and two have been under fire since the war began and are unhurt. Their letters are awfully good and the three seem very fond of their father and mother.

And now it's past twelve of the night and I'm writing this in the attic (Lightbody is away) with a bare floor and two little beds on it and the bright moon is shining straight into the window. It's only half moon but it whitens everything tonight. My light is a tiny glimmer from a primitive oil lamp and I can only just see. The guns boom accompaniment. My dear, this letter is very long and it's about nothing very exciting, but I feel the strangeness of things tonight more than I have before.

It's these things I've tried to describe to you which have impressed me and made me more pleased than ever that I'm here to live this time through and see what really is another life. I never felt death so omnipresent before. All the farms around show up as skeletons in the moonlight - you can see through their rafters and through the shell-ridden walls; and the fields are ploughed everywhere with trenches and works and filled with graves. We shelled the Germans as they left the town a month ago. There was house to house fighting to force them out, and the fields outside must be sown with corpses.

A regular told me last night in our trench that when some of these trenches were cut they came upon arms and legs and bodies of the German dead. May, the war must end before the summer. And everywhere, during the day, outside the town

---

[42]A manually-fired volley gun.

where we are in the trenches it is one incessant scream and whistle of bullets and shells and at night absolute silence between the booming of the heavy guns and the bursts of rifle fire and the machine guns.

May, I haven't written this as a sort of journal of horrors, and now I'm half in the mind not to send it. But the effect of the last five days is so strong that I feel I must try to give you some idea of it as I feel it tonight.

Please don't think I feel in the least gloomy or dispirited; I find myself looking on these things as one would watch a tragedy on the stage. They have absolutely thrilled me; I feel now I am ready for any one thing, that no circumstance of life would startle or find me altogether unprepared. And tho' in this letter it may seem as though I'm living all in shadow and gloom, really I feel as if I were passing through vivid white sheets of light and masses of dark. It seems a life of unearthly contrasts. The contrast of a searchlight beam and the dark night.

And, comrade, you'll know what it will mean, to get away from this world beyond the world and come back to you and home again, to you and our garden. My love, I can dream tonight of what our first journey into the English countryside will be like. And that English countryside shall be a symbol of our life together, beloved, you and I "they".

Farewell, dear heart,

Jack

Trenches.
Thursday.

My dear,

I got your Sunday letter this evening about five. How could I be disgusted with it my dear. It is you, and it is therefore as good as ever I want a letter. Thank you so much for getting me that sketch book and running about for it like that, but I won't pretend to be sorry you cut a lecture. How about this sore throat? My dear, you are not nearly careful enough about it yet. You are having these sore throats too often - you must preserve your throat and voice. Now I positively won't be careful out here if you don't take care too. I'm sure yours is the most dangerous foe.

I hope you are getting the various notes and letters I send. For the last week you should have one nearly every day. By the way, did you get the one with the little medal in it? And did Norman get his? I got mother's parcel yesterday and therein was a splendid cake and all sorts of other things which are turning out splendidly useful.

Comrade, it is splendid to have you there at home - it's more than I deserve. I never realised so much before that you are life to me. Without you and mother there would be nothing in life left. I find, May, that my desire to get through this business has become solely a desire to come back to you two. Do you remember Louis Stevenson in "Vagabond"? I'm so glad mother seems to keep up so well. I got a letter from father tonight too and he says mother has a bad throat too, but is keeping up well. His letter is plucky but I can tell he's really down. For their

86

sakes, May, I hope the war over as some think it will be, in two months.

I've been called out three times since I started this letter about 9 o'clock. First I had to walk down the road with the Captain and look at a communication trench, then take six men and remake parts of it that were flooded, and finally go up to headquarters to get sandbags. It's now 11.30. The Maxims[43] are going all along the line tonight and they make a fearful din. Last night was quite exciting. A sergeant and I crawled along in front of the trench to inspect the barbed wire entanglement - and it was cold - the ground all frosty and sparkling in the moonlight.

Fortunately the enemy were quiet and we got very few shots, though they must have been able to see us quite plainly. Later I took out half a dozen men to put up some fresh wire and still few shots came our way. Very considerate of the Saxons who are opposite. During the night we were shouting across to them and they to us! "how do you do," said they - many of them speak English; they wanted a game of football on Easter Monday. "Bully beef" was another cry of theirs. These "conversations" went on for quite an hour and not a shot fired. They woke up today however and plenty of sniping has gone on, and they at Maxims tonight.

I've had a promotion! I'm the 3.7 trench Howitzer Officer of "B" Coy.. We had a regular officer to instruct us this morning. It's the most primitive instrument you ever saw. It consists of a piece of iron drainpipe about 3ft. long on an iron stand at an angle of 45º. It throws a bomb about 300ft. You first drop a

---

[43]A machine gun designed by Sir Hiram Maxim.

charge of gunpowder down the barrel, then, inserting a detonator with a fuse is dropped down and finally a fuse inserted in a touch hole at the breech end, like the cannon at Waterloo! You light the fuse with a match and then run to cover, since the instrument has a knack of bursting in one's own trench. Then in preparing the bomb one has to be very careful since that too has an inclination to blow up. On the whole the weapon is a fearsome thing and I don't think "B" Coy. will worry the Germans much with trench bombs! I will not be hoist with my own petard! Still, we shot off seven bombs this morning and blew in some of their parapet.

By the way, I'm armed at last. I've got a beautiful new "short" rifle and long sword bayonet - a regular found it in a house that had been shelled and in which the owner had been killed - I'm very proud of it and it shoots splendidly. I've loosed off quite 50 rounds at Fritz[44] today. I'm wearing wet equipment and a pack and go about with a little grey wool cap in place of a cap, so altogether I think I'm becoming quite acclimatised. I've started my sketch book and by the time I come home I ought to have it full for you.

My dear, I think I've talked quite enough about myself and my doings but things are splendidly interesting here and thrilling too, sometimes. But I think three months will be quite enough - then I shall want peace and books and above all you again; May how I shall love to be with you again in English country - the idea of English peace and quiet begins to haunt me. You and I, sweetheart, with that round us and earth or any other place has

---

[44]Slang generic term for Germans.

nothing further to offer.

Goodbye, dear heart,

Jack

Friday.

My dear,

I have just got your letter - thank you ever so much for "Punch", it's splendid to have him here - it's a bit right out of England. How splendid that you and Mother and Father get on so well - Mother in her letter speaks of you "three". Of course you got on all right at the exam. After Miss Heaton's remark they don't matter a damn! At last the warm spring's come for you and you must keep well and be worthy of the time in health. Thank your people for me, please, and especially Norman for his letter. I hope he got mine and tell him I'll answer as many of his questions as soon as I can. Mother tells me you are getting that chocolate for me - thanks very much, dear. This letter is too long already and some of it too gloomy - but believe me, sweetheart, things are not really so with me and they're not to be with you -

Goodbye, comrade,

Jack

Billets.
Sunday.

My dear,

89

Thank you so much for your letter and for sending me the chocolates - I am just off to the trenches for 6 days and it will come in useful - you see it makes chocolate with hot water!

I will write you properly tomorrow when I shall have lots and lots of time. By the way I am now permanently in command of a platoon - No.8 "B" Coy. We take over a whole trench for ourselves tonight.

My love, I've no time for more but tomorrow I shall have a long talk to you.

> Goodbye dear heart,
>
> Jack

> Trenches.
> Monday afternoon.

My dear,

I've just had lunch and retired to my dug out, which I possess all to myself in virtue of my platoon commanding. It's lovely weather - bright sunshine and clear blue sky, but very cold. But before anything else, congrats. on your essay - it's splendid, dear; you ought to feel jolly bucked. Beloved, I also feel lonely, I do so want an evening alone with you again, for us to talk about everything and have our silences too. May, it is splendid to be able to look forward to years with you - and they seem so much nearer now, sweetheart. Comrade, you have made my life as splendid as the sunshine today.

I don't know whether I mentioned it in my note yesterday, but we had a smoking concert[45] in the Company on Saturday night. It was held in some school and the ceiling was pitted with shrapnel and one half of the building was a ruin and open to the sky. The weirdest, most impressive of the series of smokers I've ever been to. We had a row of candles for footlights and the same old songs for music. I thought all the time of those we had at Coll., and what was sung there and who sung; May it is the spirit which made this such a success which carries English people anywhere. They take England wherever they go and preserve it too, unchanged. I spent from 8.30 - 12.30 last night working with some of the men making our trench dry. Putting down boards to walk on and arranging them on bricks and stones in the flooded part of the trench. It was cold - the weather froze on the boards as we handled them. This morning we kept ourselves warm digging to make fresh roofs to some dug outs and we found an unexploded German shell. It was quite intact and you could see how the time fuse was set; but like so much of their ammunition it didn't work. We've really got a lot to thank Krupps'[46] bad workmanship for!

I drew all my equipment yesterday and now wear a pack and ammunition pouches like the men. Also I've got a splendid pair of waterproof waders; they come right up over the thighs and a pair of thick rubber boots fit over them. They keep every drop of wet out and they are jolly warm to sleep in.

I've such an interesting landlord and landlady in my billet and

---

[45]Smoking concerts were live performances, usually of music, before an audience of men only; popular during the Victorian era.

[46]The major German arms manufacturer.

they treat me awfully well. Café au lait in the morning and at all sorts of other times, hot water and long talks about their two sons in the firing line in the Argonne. The old lady reads me all their letters with great gusto. They both remember 1870 - 1871 and the husband was in the 3rd. Cuirassier. The people are quite keen on the men in their houses and they all turned out when we moved off to the trenches last night to wish us "bonne chance".

I never knew a place with so many cafés as our billeting town. They're called "Estaminets" and each one has its own dedication and they vary extraordinarily. One is "À la Bire Bourgeoisé" another "Au Coq Anglaise", a third to "She Barbe" and another "Aux Fleurs de Jardines". A good one is "À l'habitude"! All the officers here patronise "She Barbe" and it's really jolly nice, and you can sit there as long as you like with a 6d. glass of wine.

My dear, it is good of you to look after Mother and Father as you do and you couldn't tell me anything better than that you get on so well. With you to love and honour, dear heart, I can meet anything and I have the greatest joy in the world.

Goodbye, dear one,

Jack

Trenches
Wednesday

My dear,

I've really got nothing fresh to report - things go on just the same day by day, but the weather is dry though so cold. Thank you so much for newspaper cuttings - I need such loopholes to look out on to things outside this particular little area. And you are still keeping quite fit and not overworking? By the way, you never told me how the "At Home" went off - of which I've got the invitation in my pocket here. It seems such a relic of civilization.

By the way, I find it ever so much more interesting having a platoon of my own, am responsible for a trench and all improvements therein as well as repairs and the comfort and safety of the men. And they are a good lot of fellows, May and such a mixture. Some are from the big West End stores - Selfridges, the Army and Navy etc., some are typical Cockney workmen and others are clerks. There's one "Blower" Williams in particular from Kilburn; he'll work to further notice and keep the trench in a roar the whole time. Then, my colleen, we've got an Irishman, "pur et simple", Patrick O'Moore. The last time we were in the trenches it poured with rain and the men were soaked to the skin, and to crown it all there was no rum issued - then up spake Pat and finished his oration with "Comrades, of this day let us be sober".

My dear, I expect a letter from you this afternoon - a little talk to you for a few minutes - for that time I'm back home.

Goodbye, my love,

Jack

P.S. Will you send me out a little sketch book about 8"x4", for we are having 6 days off now. Quite time to do a lot!

Trenches.
Saturday.

My dear,

Your letter and Punch and Times came last night. Thank you so much, but most of all for your letter. By now the throat must be well! Of course you're not perturbed about the exam; just scrape and while you have the compliments you do on your teaching they don't matter.

Just before I began writing this the Brigadier General came round and I had to take him along my trench, and explain what was going on and tell him where to duck his head when the parapet was low. The day before yesterday, though I believe I've told you, a Regular brought me a rifle - one almost like the one I had in the O.T.C.. I've been practising shooting on Fritz for the last two days. For the last three there has been nothing but work - building dug outs and trenches and things. I'm not sorry to get back to billets tonight and get a rest. And it'll be a real one this time for I'm to be inoculated - that's two days' rest.

I've written Father and Mother and told them all sorts of odds and ends that'll interest them. By the way, I'm sorry I mentioned the sketch book after you had already got it for me - but it just shows how acceptable that parcel really was! Dear heart, I was so grateful for the last part of your letter, it brought back our last evening together so vividly - you seemed to be with me here. Our future together seems so much nearer now, comrade; and only a very few months ago it seemed to be years and years away. I can't say any more now, but you know, love; were we together it would be silence, after the seal between us.

94

Goodbye, beloved,

Jack

Billets.
France.

My dear,

I got your letter yesterday afternoon. You don't say anything about your sore throat so I hope it is quite well now and you are looking after yourself as if I were at home keeping guard over your health myself. You can't expect me to take care unless you do your part in that way too! I'm so glad you sent Norman's original letter, it is so much the better of the two as it is himself. I've sent him a letter to Hill Farm and a German bullet - I can't rise to a bayonet yet!

I wasn't surprised to hear R. was Jewish though I didn't think Bob was. It dawned upon me about two months ago - I think it was his name that first gave me the idea. I think I know why we felt a strange atmosphere now. Do you remember us talking about it that day we went to see them after we had spent the morning in London together? They seem to have an almost child-like implicit faith in the value of theories and be ready to carry them out to a logical conclusion without regard to the real, practical things of life around them. But their life must have a terrible background - a ghastly inhuman blackness - enough I should think to drive any sensitive nature to theories; anything so long as means change and the power to escape the terrors they've seen and lived in.

95

My dear, the "Narrow Seas"[47] have saved us from the conquering invaders. I think we owe some sanity of outlook to them. Comrade, it's splendid to think we can be barbaric English, you and I, dear heart, and long for children of our own to make our two lives one and a complete whole. With you and they and a garden for us to live in, and there is no need for the fancy splendours of some other life to make this worth living.

Last night we had a little thrill - an alarm at 11.30 pm. All of us turned out and marched to a large field just outside the town and waited with loaded rifles and supporting artillery. Nothing came, though a Zeppelin was expected, but it was weird, out there in the dark with absolute silence and all lights in the town out and no-one at all in the streets. My platoon had to mount guard an hour after the rest had turned in, and I had to post sentries at the street corners to challenge all and sundry who came by. We finished at 1 o'clock. So much for war's alarms!

It will be fine to have long letters from you, but you musn't, musn't get lonely. Go out my dear when you can, read and do anything rather than that. Above all don't work too hard and make yourself ill again. Your influence, sweetheart, should protect me from bullets if there is anything in spirit agency and I'm sure it did a day or two ago. I didn't tell you then, but I will now as I'm back again in billets. A bullet passed through my left sleeve up near the shoulder - in and out and never touched my arm! You must believe I shall come home without a scratch after that! Besides my darned tunic will be quite a good souvenir of 1915! I was walking along a road at the back of our trenches

---

[47]The English Channel.

talking to a pioneer about disinfecting a stagnant stream nearby, and I suppose a sniper just managed to see me. I don't think I shall be so near dead again - I shun the road by daylight now. At night, of course, it doesn't matter. One can go anywhere behind our lines after dark.

I'm so glad you've been to Kensington Gardens, and of course you would know Peter Pan - if you didn't recognise him, who would, you dryad? I do want a spring day with you; but at any rate we may hope for a late summer or autumn together - a warmer lonelier time even than Weald Park! And that day will want some beating - on that day some of the last barriers went down - on the day to come there will be none left.

Goodbye, dear comrade, I have your picture between two candles here at night, which is fitting, for I cannot kiss your hand.

    Jack

[This note was written on the back of an envelope.]

Dear May,

I have not been able to write. I am in charge of 240 man Company and am working 7 a.m. to 11 p.m.

Will write tomorrow.

    Jack

Billets.
Tuesday.

My dear,

Since I scribbled a note to you this morning I've found opportunity to write again. Our fate as to quarantine for this silly measles is still uncertain. Meanwhile we're cooped up in the mess and none may see us.

Now for your questions:-

Each platoon is in charge of one subaltern, so No.8 is solely mine. The only visits I get from superiors are generally at night, say about 1.30 a.m., when the Captain comes round and suddenly wants a communications trench digging or a breastwork improving, or, as on the other night, me to crawl out and inspect the barbed wire entanglements. Can you wonder if there's no love lost on such occasions, at such miserable hours of the night.

My dear, the Germans in front of us are very, very nervous and I think they never dream of an attack - we don't think they have sufficiently strong numbers either. They are afraid all night long that it is we who are going to advance and constantly send up flares and use a searchlight to make sure we're not creeping up to their lines. When the time comes I think it will be on our side that the attacks begin. Yes, we go into the same set of trenches each time - therein lies the monotony of the work. As to knowing my men - you will see that I've got to know some, and I think all, now, from my last note or two. They're all men of the

172nd Co.R.F.T.F[48]. One must write cypher to pass the Censor!

My dear, you must write to me just when you want to - of course it can't be too often; but I would have you write only when you're in the mood - you have so much to do, you musn't have to sit and write to me when you are sleepy and should be in bed. Only, dear-heart, remember when you can write, it can't be too often - you know there is nothing I look forward to more than little talks from you on paper. I wish it needn't be on paper. But, comrade, it's not for long compared with the time after.

Cigarettes now and then would be very acceptable - you've no idea how quickly they go! I leave the choice to you who are an expert!

May, it's splendid that you haven't any vacation books - a little work at the end will be quite enough - meanwhile rest, when the housekeeping will let you, and now spring has come, open air and sunshine.

Dearheart, I was down last night - it rained and the wind howled and I heard that "Empty! Empty!" too. But there is no real emptiness, love, and the fates can never make a real void. We have lived and loved, my love, and that will never be undone. We have to wait for fulfilment, but nothing can make it as though the glory had never been.

    Goodbye, comrade,

    Jack

------

[48]This reference is obscure. [Ed.]

Billets.

France.

My dear,

After all our quarantine is over! It has lasted two days and now
we are free to go back to the trenches tomorrow night and go
where we like in the meanwhile and do what we like. I got your
Sunday letter yesterday and thank you so much for that and the
picture paper. Also for the Times and the archaeological cutting
you sent me before. It's a welcome change after war, war, war!
But we are going to do the English country churches aren't we,
on our first holiday together, you and I? I'm so glad to hear you
are quite fit - but be careful you keep so - it's at the end of these
spells of housekeeping that you feel it - so beware!

Isn't it splendid that the Spring has come at last? Even here we
feel it though we're having regulation April showers. You sent
me a token of the Spring - May, I can't send one back - there are
no flowers here; but in the trenches, yes. You shall have one, my
dear.

But I do "mind about what." Sweetheart ,I think I can guess, and
since we are barbarians, will it not be the triumph of our
comradeship to come?

It seems months to me since I came out here - life has been so
crowded and thrillingly interesting. I've had to count the days to
convince myself that it's only just over three weeks since we
had that last evening together.

My love, why weren't we married first! Why should all the petty,
sordid and foolish things of life prevent our coming together
now the time is ripe? We are forced to waste two or three years

of our lives apart which would be so precious to us together, and all to pay for the codes and requirements of civilisation. But the Fates can't prevent us, while we live, being life mates - they can only hinder. We have overcome so many obstacles you and I, comrade; the remainder are small compared with those we've passed, and now we have not very far to go - a very little time ago it seemed as though a gulf of years separated us. May, it will not be long; if the war has separated us for a little while, it has shortened the time of real separation which we had to look forward to before. Once, you know, it was ten years, then five; my love, seeing that a few months of war will mean a year or two on my age, can't we hope to halve that time again?

I have so much, too my beloved, to say to you, I dare not say on paper. I want to be with again when silence would be enough and your lips on mine.

My landlord and landlady are named Percy and they live in La Rue des Jardines. Madame tells me her grandfather loved soldiering, "il etait un bon guerrier,"[49] and although he was too old to go to war in '71, '72[50] he made an application time and time again but in vain. "But my boys," she says, "they too were burning to go, c'est dans le sang[51], monsieur, n'est-ce pas?".

You must not pinch to buy books for me. You know you yourself need so many. Only now and again when there is a clear surplus are you to run to 7d's. In place of all those you don't buy you

---

[49]"He was a good soldier."

[50]The Franco-Prussian war presumably.

[51]"...it is in the blood, right?"

must write and tell me about yourself and doings and books you read.

Please thank Grace for her note and tell her we are only allowed Nestles[52] in A-------[53] so there are no clinking milkpails and no charming maids to carry them. But we have some pierrots and pierrettes[54].

 There is much to say, but not now, my dear.

> Goodbye, sweetheart,

> Jack

> Trenches.
> Wednesday.

My dear,

Your letter came this afternoon and now you are at the Presentation. I wish I could be there and at the Service at the Abbey afterwards. Last year we walked right up the Embankment afterwards, do you remember? And then I rushed back to a smoking concert given by the Principal. I wonder whether there is to be one this year. Your dinner ought to be great and you will be so splendid in your dress - my dear, I must see you in it - and is it a worthy successor to the red. But there

---

[52]Sterilized milk in cans.

[53]Name of town censored.

[54]French pantomime characters with whitened faces, white costumes, and pointed hats – Jack is jesting methinks.

is to be another red, isn't there - and that on the most wonderful of all occasions we shall have yet had together. My love, that will be the first of many.

I am so glad to hear you are going to use my room to work in - it will be so much quieter and better than having to read right on the noisy street. But please don't read all my books, leave me just one or two to be superior about!

Do you know I am getting to be quite an ignoramus - I am forgetting everything - yesterday I couldn't even remember the name of the great hall in "Beowulf." To comfort myself I wrote up in charcoal over my "dug-out" the only chorus in Old English.

[Here Jack has written the chorus in Anglo Saxon, reproduced below.]

"*Þæs oferēode swa þisses mæg*".

Will you send me out my edition of "Beowulf," the little brown one, so I can go through it these afternoons when things are quiet and I have nothing better to do?

My dear, I have nothing fresh to tell you today. I am trying to write a series of little pictures of situations that have impressed me and I will send them on to you if I can make them worth reading. One shall describe some of my men - I'm sure you'll be keen on some of them. After the war you really must meet them - especially Macleod. You know I'm very proud of them.

My dear, dear girl, you musn't worry too much over me; I shall come back, I feel certain, and I want you so. The thought of seeing you again, love, of being with you is the most precious thing I have. My comrade, that will take me through everything to the end of this time apart. Then, dear heart, my life, our life, begins.

Goodbye comrade,

Jack

Trenches.
Saturday.

My dear,

I got your Tuesday evening letter yesterday for which much thanks. It's a pity Ted goes away like that. He is in rather a bad way I think to have such a fixed idea that he is not coming back. The hope for him is the bustle and life he'll get out in Egypt. I think there's a very fair chance of it being at any rate something of a cure. Of course he hasn't anyone to write him letters like that.

So you have started going to the dentist's again - when will he be done?

I have come across Raphael's theory of a poet before, but I can't make up my mind where, but I fancy it was in the criticism of Francis Thompson. I believe it is applicable to some - say Shelley, or, to very much less degree, Byron, but I don't believe it can be generalised. In many cases it is the poet's great joy of life that is behind all his work and which is only understandable by the few. And a poet's work will so reflect and be coloured with that aspect which most exhilarates him and rouses the keenest interest in him. I rather think that a large part of this theory of gloom and universal sadness rests on much the same basis as that of the "Gentlemen of France" (do you remember in King John?)[55] who were sad for wantonness.

This theory is the result, I suppose, of pessimism of some natures - the decadents I believe. In some say in Thomas Hardy himself of Louis Stevenson, the hard cruel things of life rouse a fighting spirit in them and in the latter, specially, a splendid joy in life. They have no use for purposeless sadness - that means a complete giving up of personal effort and therefore loss of individuality and finally, I am convinced loss of all power of doing whatsoever. It's the same spirit that inspires some of our paling minor poets who fill dainty velvet bound volumes with series of short moans, all copied from Continental prototypes, and really more inane than their originals because their authors haven't even had energy enough to give up trying on their account or to compose their own "Lamentatio" but have cribbed their agonies from others all ready made. Granted the world is cruel and the universe empty - why can't these people be content with Omar in the verse that goes -

And that inverted bowl we call the sky[56] -

Thomas Hardy is the same - they have found the cruel realities of life - they have shown them and all that remains for them is

---

[55] Shakespeare, King John Act IV, scene I "Yet, I remember, when I was in France, Young gentlemen would be as sad as night, Only for wantonness."

[56] From *Omar Khayyam's Rubaiyat* (st. 72), (FitzGerald's translation) : "And that inverted Bowl we call The Sky, Whereunder crawling coop't we live and die, Lift not thy hands to it for help -- for It Rolls impotently on as Thou or I."

to make a good fight to the end. It's the spirit of "And man's forgiveness give and take[57]."

Of this theorising enough!

Has Grace heard from Clements? Whether he is in the fighting line or not, and if so how he's getting on? I had a letter from King - you remember him and his sister at King's? He is out here with an ammunition column and within sound of the guns and seems to be enjoying himself.

You ought to have had the two weeks off from Greycoat - you want more rest from teaching than you are getting now - I should think the College is paying your fare. It will be a splendid thing when the Diploma business is over and you can really start teaching. Only you'll work too hard unless you are constantly on the lookout over yourself.

Make the most of the Spring - and there really shouldn't be any "if" about your going away this Easter. You ought, you must find somewhere to go into the country. And please tell me if there are expenses and to what they run. You know I'm quite rich - there must be nearly £50 in Cox's for me now!

By the way you never told me how the "At Home" went that I should have been at - I've got the invitation in my pocket now - my last relic of civilisation! And you really had a good time at Thornton Heath? It's a pity you can't have such weekends at least once a month. You must consider this idea - I'm sure it's a

---

[57] *Ibid.* (st. 81 (later ed.)) "Oh Thou, who Man of baser Earth didst make, And ev'n with Paradise devise the snake; For all the Sin wherewith the Face of Man Is blackened - Man's forgiveness give and take!"

good one!

Over five pages, it is enough!

Goodbye, dear girl,

Jack

Trenches,
France.

My dear May,

I have just got your Wednesday evening letter. Really it should have come up here yesterday, but there was some confusion and it was not brought up till this morning. Thanks so much for "Punch" - isn't it splendid this week - I think one of the best I remember. Thanks, too, for the chocolate - I look forward to it!

Unfortunately the measles scare prevented me being inoculated - I shall have to wait 5 days now.

I'm glad Grace has heard from Clem - I'm not surprised he's not cheerful about the casualties - unfortunately we've had a considerable number and, May, it's horrible to see - I think I shall never get used to standing by these cases - and I'm sure I'll never forget. There were three yesterday - one a bad one - all from shrapnel. Fortunately only one has been wounded in my platoon and that was before I came out. The three yesterday were in the trench next to me and they were brought through my trench. I supplied the brandy.

Last night I took my platoon out in front of the parapet digging - the Germans were considerate again and gave us very few shots. But my men were splendid - I never knew better workers and such a cheerful, merry lot, too. There are two labourers, and they love digging and building "dugouts", two carpenters, a plumber, half a dozen shop assistants and some clerks. The whole lot work, play and share together. Oh, then I've a lance corporal who in private life writes music hall sketches, songs and topical poems. He's done several this week or two, and jolly good they are too. I'll send you a copy if I can get one.

I have not been able to get any spring flowers yet; but I hope to when we go into advanced trenches tomorrow night.

Father and mother seem to have had a good time and the "Swift"[58] to have served them well. You must learn to drive, my dear.

Yes, it will be over, this business, one day, and I believe now, May, it will be comparatively soon. Everyone out here hopes so and many think so too.

By the way, in the last "Punch" you sent, there was a description under the title of "The Watchdogs" of fresh troops coming up into the firing line. It's one of the finest descriptions I've seen and in very many of the details it might refer to the town here. In fact I'm half inclined to think it does.

Really, I've got more to do than write letters, though you may not think so by the length of this - therefore till tomorrow, goodbye,

Jack

---

[58]A popular make of car at the time.

P.S.   (1) Not too much work during the Easter vac!

(2) I am very keen on hearing that you have made progress in the cuisine. I would pass judgement!

Sunday evening.

Before I sent off this morning's letter I got yours of Friday morning. The chocs. and cigarettes will be very acceptable and thanks.

You ought to be very proud of the way you make friends with small children, especially small boys; they are very good judges and jolly good critics. But I've said this so many times.

May, it was not mad for you to say what you have said about marriage; your letters have meant so much to me since I have been out here and made me feel you very, very near me. It is I who have said too much and want forgiveness.

The real reason why you are "dangerous" is a very nice one - you remember I have often pointed out the compliments that are always being paid to you by all sorts and conditions of people? These make up the reason.

Again, goodbye

Jack

Tuesday,
Trenches.

Dear May,

I am in the Advance trenches and have just had a night's work and am now going on to drain my "dugout" which is at present drowned. However it's fine and one doesn't mind working.

Still on this point there is nothing to report, and fortunately no more casualties. Your two parcels of chocs. haven't arrived yet, but I believe they are at the Orderly Room, and through some confusion they have not been brought up here. I expect them today and smack my lips! I also expect a letter from you - but that won't be until 5 or 6 o'clock this evening. And you are still well? That throat musn't have too many lapses, you know.

The orderly is waiting to go to town with the letters - therefore no more. I must write to you properly later so you get it tomorrow.

>Goodbye, my dear,

>Jack

>Tuesday afternoon,
>Trenches.

My dear,

Your box has just come - thank you so much - they're the first Turkish cigarettes I've had since I came out - they are a treat. And it's sunny Spring here today, with a lark singing. Why aren't you and I together out in English country today! But anon, and soon, too!

I'm afraid I've written you dull letters lately - but for some reason I've been foolishly depressed - it must have been the cold and rain; but it's gone now, Spring has come and even now it seems impossible here.

I've been so busy this last few days that time has flown and if it doesn't one gets so tired of rows and rows of sandbags and wet earth and low "dugouts."

Yesterday we had a little diversion. Two German and two British aeroplanes were over us at once and the sky was literally filled with bursting shells - over a hundred were counted at one time. One of the Germans was hit, but he got back to his own lines. We heard today that another had been brought down in our "Billets" town itself. The change of pencil in this letter was due to my rushing out to see if a passing biplane was English or German. If it is an enemy we all fire and drive him off - otherwise he finds our range and shells come over later. It was British.

And you - you are still well and not too busy? And is the Spring really come to England yet? To keep you happy and well?

But there will be a letter tomorrow, till then, dear heart, goodbye,

    Jack

P.S. The chocs. are splendid.

Trenches,
Thursday.

My dear,

Your letter came last night and thank you so much. This I expect will be a day late for we go out tonight back to billets and the letters of today don't go off till tomorrow night. Then there's Sunday in between.

Dear girl, I do wish I could be with you, that we could go out and talk, and have the Spring together. I am so sorry about Miss Westlake; but, beloved, only you and I understand and the rest will talk. Only you must not let them worry you, we can afford to keep our own counsel and plan our own life in our own way. Ever since we came together no-one has understood how much we depend on one another, nor how we love May, we have the Fates to thank that they never have. They would have us calmly reckon up each other and consider suitable points and reasons. Meanwhile, comrade, I know that without you I am nothing and with you I want our life to the uttermost. I cannot say any more, dear one; but how much you mean to me here, how splendid you have made life for me and how much I want you, you know.

Billets,
Friday.

We were relieved last night about 8 o'clock and it was such a glorious Spring day and starlit night. We got back without any casualties though some wretched sniper had ten shots at us when we were half way home. There are civilians living in the neighbourhood who are in the pay of the Germans and hide behind hedges at night and wait for parties of soldiers as they go to and from the trenches. We are going to try and catch this particular one next time we go up. The Germans in front of us were very quiet this time - in fact we could hardly get a shot out of them and we could work in front of our parapet at night and on top of it with little danger.

At present I have nothing to do with the 3.7 Howitzer (otherwise the drainpipe cannon) for the R.F.A.[59] have brought up one of their own, and a much better one, which they use to some purpose.

As usual No.8 Platoon worked splendidly - most of the day and night and they seem to like it. There's one man especially, Reed, a general labourer at home, who is never content unless he is building dug-outs or parapets or cooking. The other night I was asking the time and he remarked that the last time he had seen his watch it was with a rich relative - his uncle in fact! He tells me he is one of five brothers and they're all at the front. Then there's another who is a Commissioner of the Bedford Level[60], owner of several bootshops, landowner in Ely and above all a godson of Disraeli. Of the last he's enormously proud. Talking to a Lance Corporal last night, I found that he was a Met.[61] conductor between Aldgate and Baker Street. You may have seen him, and so may have we!

May, before I came out I wanted to buy you your hood and gown - may I do it now, please?

I'm so glad you're going to have a frock from Miss Wells - it's so much more likely to be worthy of you - and it has some red! Of course you have decided by now to go to Horsmonden[62] -

---

[59]Royal Field Artillery.

[60]Also known as The Great Level of the Fens; the largest region of fen in Eastern England.

[61]The Metropolitan Railway, part of the London Underground.

[62]Horsmonden is a village in Kent, on the Weald. Gypsy horse fairs were held on the large village green each year until recent years.

cheers! It will be just splendid for you. Years ago I remember getting a book out of the Library to find out where it was and all about it - you went there almost directly after you came to see me that first time - that's two years ago. By the way couldn't it be a fortnight?

Do you know I've had a note from Cox's to say I've got £90 in the bank. My dear you will remember this won't you, when you want various things you ought to have?

I am expecting your letter by today's mail, and till it comes, goodbye sweetheart and comrade.

Jack

P.S. (1) You were right about London Opinion[63] - it's jolly good.

(2) I am reading Ivan Tourgeneff[64] 'une mechée de gentilshommes'[65], am I not civilised?

Billets,
France.

My dear,

Your letter came yesterday and the chocolate from Fullers. Now you're really in Kent and in your right surroundings for the

---

[63]A popular periodical of the time.

[64]Ivan Sergeyevich Turgenev (November 9 [O.S. October 28] 1818 – September 3 [O.S. August 22] 1883), Russian realist novelist.

[65]'A Nest of Gentlefolk' (1859)

Spring. My love, thank you so much for your letter - I too do not want to live on memory only - and letters are all we can have for a little time. Now your letters stand for those times we had together and they bring me you in spirit. But, beloved, I dream of and long for the time when we can have done with memories and the ghosts of kisses; I want you so to talk to me and be by me; above all to have those silences and the magic of you. There is no need for words then, we cannot talk, so much more is conveyed by touch, by your caress.

Three years, dear one, are long; but they will be so short - after this.

There is no excuse for influenza after Kent - you must keep well from now till I come home, and of course after; but mind, never a lapse henceforth!

Yes please, directly the socks are finished; but not too much knitting - there are so many things for you to do in Spring and so much fresh air and sunshine waiting for you.

Here things go on steadily almost unchangingly. Last night I went to the "Follies" - a permanent entertainment run by a party of soldiers (professionals in private life) with the assistance of two French girls. And one of the latter sang "Gilbert the Filbert" with a very French accent. What a contrast to the Palace! But I think I prefer our own smoking concerts - and some of our own men sing very well - and there is far less of the Music Hall.

I was glad to get the Weekly edition of the Times - it gives you a connected account of the week's happenings - thanks very much for sending it. No, the casualties marked do not refer to

115

us. I don't think any of ours have appeared yet. The double number of "Punch" was jolly good - and it had my favourite in - " Will you have your bath before or hafter l'action, Sir?"

So the war can't even leave our Psychology man alone - Louvain[66] isn't the only Library it has harmed.

We've been on the range (one we built ourselves) practising shooting at sniping plates all the morning and at 2.30 we go on a route march. Such is our rest! We return to trenches tomorrow night - to some new ones so it means more hard work building parapets etc. etc.. By the way I am rather bucked because I find the whole company envies No 8 Platoon - as the best of the bunch. That's two of that name! Really my dear the chocs. weren't frivolous - they were just lovely in the trenches - no more frivolous than you are, my lady - and a compliment would follow, but you will guess it and it's not good enough for you.

Goodbye comrade, you make me want so much to deserve my title,

> Jack

> Billets,
> Saturday.

My dear,

---

[66]Capital of the province of Flemish Brabant in Flanders, Belgium. The university library was deliberately destroyed by the German army on August 25, 1914.

116

I have had two letters from you on two successive days and a "Punch". Thank you so much; and especially for your "Bonne Chanson"[67] - "The rare song for singing the fine song to hear." "de ceux qui s'aiment sans mélange[68]," and the splendour of it, dear one, it is ours. My love it will be also a battle song.

I am glad you go to see Mother and Father often and Mother can be your friend. I dared not hope you two, my two, would come together so soon. In the greatest of all things, comrade, I am rich beyond most.

Today I went to be inoculated and now I look forward to two days real slacking and time to read my Russian book and write letters. Lewis' note is quite characteristic from the losing of my address to the promise of an introduction! And he is so anxious lest I catch cold!

I have changed my billet (parceque les insectes invisibles![69]) and am now in a chemist's - a mother and son. They are awfully nice - the son was a student at Lille University before the war and is expecting to go with the French Ambulance in May. Madame his mother is charming and spoils me with coffee and wines red and white and all sorts of kindness. I've been treated awfully well since I've been here - in fact since I left Southampton.

I was afraid you would have to make a series of visits to the

---

[67] A series of poems written by the French poet, Symbolist leader, and Decadent Paul-MarieVerlaine to his wife Mathilde.
[68] "Of those who love each other without reserve."
[69] "Because of invisible insects," presumably bedbugs.

dentist's again for tooth stopping; and it is such a rotten process. But twice is quite enough - now no more for months!

Your Latin pupil has just followed suit with the rest of those who have known you and paid you fitting compliments. I am glad she knew so well as to bring you a little piece of Spring and the Country.

Concerning the Head and the rest of the school - I've said "I told you so" so many times bluntly and politely that I dare not again, though you see I've managed it really!

My dear, you must not worry about me - I am quite fit and well, and ever so careful not to catch cold in the trenches as Lewis thinks I might. Be you so too.

Are you sure it can't be more than a week at Horsmonden? Try to make it a fortnight, please.

There is nothing more to report,

> Goodbye dear heart,
>
> Jack

Billets,
France.

My dear,

The post orderly is just going - therefore my note must be of the briefest --

So far, and this is the third day I have not felt the slightest effect from inoculation - I don't think I shall now. Three of the officers from Epsom have come out - and are posted to our company - my old captain is also coming -

No more till tomorrow -

Yours,

     Jack

I hope you're having weather like it is here for Horsmonden.

Trenches,
Thursday.

My dear,

We came in again last night with absolutely no adventures. This time we are in some new breastworks and they are beautifully dry, high and clean - and with the real Spring weather life is worth living.

But my dear, I've got a splendid sergeant just come back from hospital of the name of Macleod. He's the son of an Indian judge and as mad as a hare, though awfully useful and full of ideas and energy. We two went out last night to prospect the German front and we have plans against their snipers and listening post. Of this, more anon. Unfortunately he is likely to get a commission and I shall lose him.

And the Kent country - it's in your last letter which came yesterday and it's so splendid to get a breath of it here. Oh, my love, that wandering holiday together! So much of the joy of the "Four Men" and not the gloom of the ending. We shall have so much more than they and all the world and life before us.

So far there is no more to tell, but we've six days here probably so there ought to be more anon.

The best of the Spring and the country be yours love,

Goodbye comrade,

Jack

France,
Friday.

My dear one,

I have just got your letter and postcard, they have thrilled me. You give me, my love, the greatest of all things. I want no more of life than to be with you and to love and honour you, the one woman in the world for me and as queen to stand for all.

Since, May, you have been so splendid a comrade, dear, have taught me so many things that for the rest I lived on dreams which I dared not think would fail to come true, but which, until so little time ago, I thought were years hence. The letter which you brought me to tell me you needed me, the first time I kissed you, those days at Harrow and in the Forest, and greatest of all, in Weald Park[70] - my love the thrill of those was marvellous enough and they made life for me and you make it still. For the rest, May, I understand - our future can never seem common or

---

[70]Weald Country Park, Essex. At nearly 500 acres it is the largest of the Essex County Council Country Parks.

ordinary or stale, you stand for womanhood to me - the greatest thing of all, my queen.

Yesterday afternoon I spent some time sniping from a plate at the Germans and I think I managed to worry them. You see we have square iron plates put in the parapet with a hole just big enough to put a rifle through and they form jolly good loopholes. After putting several through the German sniping hole opposite me and splitting the sandbags round about I got a reply - and this was rather too good. It caught the stock of my rifle and sent the splinters and pieces of earth through my loophole and they caught my left hand slightly. However, very little damage was done and after getting it dressed by the stretcher bearers, to whom I went, I walked down to the Field dressing station and got it seen to again.

I returned to the trench but the Captain insisted on my going down to see the Medical Officer in the evening and so spoiled my plans with Sergeant Macleod of which I told you. As a result I am now in Hospital for a day or two in order to get my hand clean of the grit and little splinters. I have had an anti-tetanus injection and am now at peace with the world. I expect to be quite capably lefthanded again in a day or two. I have given you all this rigmarole so that you may understand that very little indeed is the matter with me and that I am not making things appear better than they are.

You will also be prepared to laugh when my name appears in the casualty list, as I am afraid it will. I have tried to stop it, but the R.A.M.C.[71] are bound by red tape and must enter up every

---

[71] Royal Army Medical Corps.

case however small. At present of course, my hand has a plum pudding appearance, but in all I should think there are hardly a dozen small cuts and scratches, though much bandage.

Please, I was not careless.

Thanks, about the food, I am sending the cheque (uncrossed) in a registered envelope tomorrow. Don't you think "cheque" sounds magnificent? The loss per week is a pity, but you will not have so much chance of overworking, and that is worth a lot you scamp! Raphael sent me such a lot of "Three Castles" cigarettes - wasn't it good of him? I'm writing to them both tomorrow.

By the way I didn't thank Norman for his letter - I will write to him also à demain[72] and in case my father hasn't delivered up the bullet, enclose another. I shall be glad to hear about the church and will return learned comments, almost certain to be wrong, but learned!

By the time you get this, my dear, you will be back in London - and well. You must try seriously to keep so for me when I come back; and I really think that will not be very long, though a soldier remarked the other day that he thought the first five years of the war would be the worst. My songwriter has made a burlesque "Fifty Years in the Trenches" and as an old man of eighty complains that when attacking the German trenches in a bombing party his beard gets caught in their "barbed wire". Tonight enough.

---

[72]Tomorrow.

Farewell comrade, and my love you also know.

Jack

France,
Sunday.

My dear,

I am sending you the cheque for 30/- in a registered envelope and I hope there will be no difficulty. I still feel rather chary of cheques and inwardly wonder whether the Bank is going to accept my signature etc. etc.. I haven't got used yet to being Croesus[73]. And now you are back in London again and well and still enjoying the Spring. Here it is April also but there seem to be no flowers - no primroses or the like though there was a lovely box sent to the Hospital. I think they came from somewhere in France.

As for myself I am living on the fat of the land and getting fearfully lazy. My hand is ever so much better - almost clean now and I expect to go up to the trenches tomorrow afternoon. While I was away our artillery gave them five minutes rapid shrapnel fire and our men blazed off rapid rifle fire. The sergeant I spoke about got so excited that he jumped up on top of the parapet to fire at the Germans. Luckily he wasn't hit nor did we have any casualties. Of course it would be my luck not to be there, but I expect we shall repeat the experiment later on.

There is in my room one other patient, an interpreter of the

---

[73]As in, "as rich as Croesus."

123

French Army, and lecturer at Birmingham University. He knows Spiers of King's and Salmon and all sorts of other notables. As a non-commissioned officer he would salute me on parade - one of the horrors of war! This last day or two the Germans have taken to shelling the Town but very little damage has been done. They're doing it now and making a terrible noise.

By the way I haven't been able to get Norman another souvenir yet since they are all packed away and I shan't be able to get at them until tomorrow. Then he shall have one.

My dear one, it was a splendid idea to send me the postcard of the "eponymous ancestor"; your royalty and so fitting now, and it brought back old times so vividly. And they <u>are</u> worth bringing back, love.

I think Westminster will always be a shrine for us - we have learnt so many things there together, you and I, comrade. All our lives it will be a storehouse for us in which I think we shall always find peace.

> Goodbye dear heart,

> Jack

Trenches

Tuesday.

My dear,

You see I am back again - I came yesterday afternoon for I was so tired of being in the town while the company was in the Front. My hand progresses well - I helped to put out some barbed wire last night which is proof enough - and I expect it will be quite right by the time we go up again in 6 days.

I got your drawing and letter - thank you so much - and it did bring English country and its quiet along with it. I haven't time now to talk about the Rood Stair and the other good things you tell me of - but this evening after we come out there will be. I am looking forward to thinking over your letter and sketch tonight. And dear, the sketch is good - really. Please send me some more if you have time and inclination to do any.

By the way, I met an old Shaftsbury Boy in the street here - in the R.A.M.C. - and he tells me that Hudson (do you remember him at the Tech.?) is in billets in the Town. I am going to seek him out.

Till tonight, love, goodbye,

Jack

P.S. (1) I too, my dear, have a keepsake with a little red "M". (2) My hand goes excellently - I have only one finger bound up now. (3) Thanks very much for the "Times" and L.O. It's good to have the whole week's news together.

Billets,
France.

My dear one,

At last I can sit down and write to you properly and think about the churches and all the things you have told me in your last letters. I got your postcard only today along with your letter

125

from home.

As far as I can see the church seems to have had perpendicular windows inserted in place of its dec.[74] e.g. in the N. aisle. The door looks like an Augustan refurbishing and so does the stone work round the three light window in the Tower though the windows themselves might have been dec.. The top (small) window was evidently originally a two light dec. and the mullions having decayed, they just put in that black shutter only just leaving the two points of the arches showing above.

The tower itself I should think is dec. period. The West window of the South Aisle looks like a fine specimen of dec. tracery though perhaps the tracery is a modern copy?

Those two "roodstairs" in your drawing are very interesting and so is the theory about one being used for the platform for the Passion Plays. But these usually took place in the chancel and were hardly elaborate enough, I thought, to need a stage while they were played in the churches themselves. Later of course when the guilds (?) played them outside it was different.

In the little book "The Growth of the English Church" there's a photograph of an "Easter Sepulchre" in the chancel where it's thought the "Cross" was "buried" when the Easter passion play was performed. But then in such cases the theatrical element in the "Play" was very limited, just two or three clerics taking the prominent characters and the choir acting as a sort of chorus and singing "responses".

I wondered whether at one time there was a Chantry Chapel cut

---

[74]Decorated Period (1280-1380).

off from the rest of the Church by wooden screen-work as they often were in conjunction with these screens. There's a very good example at Dennington near Framlingham[75] which we shall be able to see when we have our holiday there together. The door more to the East may have been for the Rood Screen proper and the other for the "chantry" screen.

But probably the "stage" theory has very good authority and would knock mine flying. Anyhow, it's nice to have these things to think of here and especially to be able to talk them over with you. How splendid it will be after words for us to be able to go and see these places together in the Spring and Summer and go on to Rye. My love, we shall really wander in the world beyond the world, you and I.

Today it is exactly 6 weeks since I saw you and to me also it seems so long; and I have had so much in that time to make it fly. Dear heart, I wish I could be with you. Days become almost hours for me then, and for me, love, nothing is grey. Together I feel we can go through life and defy the "prison shades", as R.L.S. did.

Goodbye, comrade,

Jack

Trenches.

My dear,

Your letter and "Times" have just come to hand - thank you ever

[75]A pretty Suffolk village.

so much for both. I should think the Rackham "Peter Pan" was fine and a present worth giving.

You know, it's rather good for 1/4 of a Music Hall show to be amusing for it's a bit more than they usually manage, I think.

May, it's splendid to think of you at home, I couldn't want more than that you should be with Mother - it's one more thing I've got to be grateful to you for. My love, what a splendid prelude to the time when you will be a "daughter of the house", and they will be our people. Comrade, I can never tell you enough how you have made my life and given it the very best it could hold.

May, there are many things I can tell you which I don't think I ought to let them know at home - till after the war. You see Mother would think of them so much they would become magnified enormously and be ever present with her. The following is an instance.

The night before last I went out with Macleod and a private to look at a wagon standing in front of the German lines, in which we thought there was a sniper. We crawled out about 250 yds. along the side of a ditch - very, very cautiously and lay and watched. But there was no sniper - only German shells came flying overhead, though of course they couldn't do us any harm.

To make sure I then crawled on for 20 yds. or so and just as I got flat on the ground the "Bosches"[76] sent up a flare which fell quite close to me - of course they saw me and when I turned to go back to the other two, shots began to come our way, though you know it is very difficult to aim in the dark with any

---

[76]A slang word for Germans.

certainty so there wasn't really very much danger.

We all slid into the ditch and then a machine gun opened fire on us, or rather where they thought we were. We slowly made our way down the ditch, and the mud and water came up over the thighs, and the Germans, thoroughly alarmed, for they could hear our splashing as we went, sent up flares and rattled off with rifles and machine gun.

Half way down the ditch was a bridge, and here they thought we should have to come out of the ditch and crawl along to pass, so they set the machine gun on it. Fortunately they were wrong - there was about 2 ft. between the top of the water and the top of the bridge, so we could just get through and make our way right to our own trench, accompanied with flares and musketry.

So worried were the Germans that they sent up a red flare which is a signal to their own men an attack is expected! There's quite a "Three Musketeers" touch about that, isn't there? But we cost them quite a lot in ammunition etc. and quite annoyed them.

More than this there has been little happening - we had some fifteen shells over two nights ago, two of which slightly damaged the trench but there was no harm done. Since we've been up I think there have been two casualties in the whole Battalion. You know we're nearly as safe as you who cross London streets daily.

I started to write to you yesterday and then I thought I wouldn't say anything about the other night's affair, but since your letter I've changed my mind. In its way it's quite interesting - but really not <u>nearly</u> as dangerous as it seems. Four pages and really there is no news! Can I not also gossip?

Goodbye, dear, and the best of the Spring be yours.

Jack

P.S.(1) My hand is quite healed now - I was shown my name in the casualty list this morning - one of the comedies of War! (2) I got a paper and letter from your father yesterday - for which please thank him for me. I must write too, and also to Norman.

Trenches.

My dear,

I got your Tuesday letter yesterday. How silly of the W.O.[77] to send a telegram like that - I'm so sorry you did not get my letter before. You see I went into hospital late on Thursday night and I couldn't get the things to write with until after the post had gone on Friday morning.

And you are still well and content? I hope you've got the weather we have here - it's simply real Spring. The meadows behind the trenches we're in now are one mass of yellow and white and the fruit trees in the ruined farm gardens are in bloom. Yesterday I heard the cuckoo for the first time - only a few yards away in some trees.

Really my dear, Macleod is a very useful man and I'd rather be out at night with him than anyone. He is not the sort who would

---

[77]War Office.

get jumpy and let off his gun at awkward moments or do things like that.

Yesterday night the Germans managed to drop three shells, out of some 15 fired, into our trench, but the damage they did was slight and there were no casualties. These are awfully good trenches and will stand any amount of shell fire.

While the weather lasts I think, on the whole I would rather be in the trenches than in billets. I scarcely ever sleep comfortably in the town because I expect to be called up with an alarm every night I hear the gunfire; here the guns boom all night and one doesn't notice it.

My beloved, these days of sunshine make me feel it only a matter of weeks, or a month or so before I see you again - I dream of it at night.

Goodbye dear heart,

Jack

P.S. Thanks again for the Times and the O. - they're just the thing here to sit and read these hot afternoons.

PART FOUR

APPENDICES

REQUIESCANT IN PACEM

On Sunday April 25th. 1915 Jack was wounded and died of these wounds on Friday May 7th. 1915. He was 22 years old.

Lieut. John Richardson.

◆

1893—1915.
Killed in Action.

[Student of English at King's College; he left unfinished a thesis on " Albion's England " —the Elizabethan patriotic poem—in preparation for the M.A. degree of the University. When recovering from a previous wound, he asked that his copy of the Old English epic " Beowulf " might be sent him from home. The refrain from the oldest English lyric " Deor's Lament," which may be rendered, " O'er that *he* triumphed, o'er this may *I* !" was chalked by him in Old English on the wall of his trench.]

Jack's obituary in The Observer newspaper

Thine was no pedant's zeal : the Mother-
 ·tongue
Taught thee high dictates of thy Fatherland ;
The call no patriot-heart can e'er withstand
Tore thee from lays by ancient poets sung.
  Well didst thou learn the lore, to thee
    endear'd,
Of that young warrior who with dragons
    fought
And conquer'd—steadfast, selfless, un-
    afear'd—
" Better is Death than Life with self-scorn
    fraught."
  Not less thy courage, though thy scholar-
    soul
Illum'd thy trench with mystic runes—the
    hope
That solac'd in his plight our oldest Scôp
Whose song is wrought on Britain's golden
    scroll.
  No greater meed wouldst thou, no prouder
    fame :
In " Albion's England " is enshrined thy
    name !

       I. GOLLANCZ.
King's College, London.

         ***

The poem printed with Jack's obituary

WHEN WAR WAS DECLARED – BY JACK

Just six months ago we were at the annual Training Camp of the Officers Training Corps attached to our University. It was near a small place called Ludgershall on the edge of the great Plain, and a blessed change it promised to be, from the round of lectures and reading which made up the University year. It is true that everyone grumbled fiercely when it was first known that the camp was to be on Salisbury Plain; it was not anticipated that this year would compare favourably with the last camp at Ilkley among the moors; but that was truly incomparable; a camp to dream of and to be a tradition for years.

The desolation of Salisbury, its utter isolation from the joys of town, these and other demerits were dwelt upon by ancient members of the Corps who were at a camp there years previously. But it was the first experience for many of us and Salisbury held no terrors; we went with a light heart, cheerful excitement and heavy kitbags. And we found the situation of the Camp was not so bad, on the slope of a hill overlooking miles of hilly country on the one hand, and the green expanses of the Plain on the other. A week of hard work followed, hard work on the open, windy plain under a blazing sun.

So we played at soldiers, learning something of the trade incidentally and enjoyed life; but the emergency for which we prepared seemed so far off, so impossible. That we, students in an English university who belonged to this Officers Training Corps, because we liked rifle shooting, and the fortnights' annual camp, should ever be called upon to be real soldiers and meet a real foe, either on our own soil or abroad, this was ludicrously remote, impossibly fantastic.

But towards the end of the week rumours came that affairs on the Continent were becoming serious and we listened with hardly mild interest. We had heard it all before; then our captain spoke of three hundred of us being wanted if required by the Government should things become worse. "But they won't" we mentally noted and played on. Next we heard war was inevitable between Germany and Russia; war, then, was becoming an actuality, and a Continental war too. Some of the play went out of Camp.

Someone remarked that the Adjutant looked worried and he was decidedly short on the early morning parade. Could it be that affairs were getting really critical for this country, we questioned? We heard that France was embroiled, Belgium, and, incredible news, England. Here was reality. The long discussed catastrophe, so long discussed that it had as much reality to us as scientific prophecies of the end of the world, was dangerously threatening. The sing-songs in the canteen had lost three quarters of their 'go'.

I was on guard that Saturday evening, and on sentry go near enough to the canteen to hear the merriment inside. Suddenly there was a hush. An evening paper had come declaring that war, yes war, had become almost inevitable, that England must fight, was on the eve of mobilisation. The Chaplain read it out to the audience and sobered even that careless throng. Thereafter the Camp was silent. On the Sunday morning the Captains came round and took the names of volunteers for Commissions, and practically all of us gave in our names.

There was a meeting in the Canteen where the Adjutant presided, and we cheered some half dozen who went up to the table and gave in their names for commissions in the Regular Army. This was a new experience then that has now become so much a matter of course. In turn we all filed up and wrote our names in a book, and gave particulars in case we were wanted.

The rest of the day was spent in gloom; little knots of men discussing over and over again the incredible news. That evening two of us went for a long ramble in the quiet lanes and little villages, which seemed to bear an added charm and doubled peace that night in view of the troubles ahead. The last Sunday of peace in England for who knows how long, the last Sunday that one could legitimately enjoy the quiet splendour of the English country-side, perhaps for years. We were lost that evening and only got back to Camp long after 'lights out' had sounded, and the Guard had to be evaded by help of the dark edge of an adjoining wood.

There was a wild rumour that two dreadnoughts had been sunk in the North Sea; then it's war at last, we thought. We had hardly gone to sleep before we were roused by the noise of a motor bicycle driving into the Camp next to us. Then bugles were heard sounding, and cries, and creeping out of the tent we saw that our neighbours were striking Camp by lantern light. But we had no sign and after some time went back to sleep. In the morning everybody was on a strain with excitement, but there was battalion drill as usual before breakfast.

After, however, the order came to strike Camp and two hours of hard work followed, with a march to the neighbouring barrack town of Tidworth, and a whole day unloading the lorries bringing in the impediments of our Camp. And there were dozens of such lorries and wagons all bringing in material from the camps on the Plain. At last we were finished and marched to our train to return to London. The journey took hours and all along the line we saw trucks carrying horses and red-cross wagons and guns and all the stuff of war. We sung our choruses on the station platforms where we had to wait to keep up our spirits. We bought evening papers which declared we should be at war in twenty four hours, at war, overpowering thought, with Germany.

Here, then, was this impossible event which had been foretold so many times, that we had grown careless of the reiterated cry of 'Wolf'. Again, war with Germany, with the strongest European power, was inevitable - we only waited the repudiation of our twenty four hour ultimatum and the guns would be brought to bear and the great ships cleared for action. We were subdued, preoccupied and silent during the journey home, cheered here and there by other passengers on the line, realising that after all even in the twentieth century, we, university students, must fight for our lives, for our homes and country.

Twenty four hours later war was declared, and now it is six months ago and men have fought and died by their thousands and hundreds of thousands. Our losses are now nearing one hundred and five thousand, and at least a dozen of those who played at soldiers on Salisbury Plain are dead by Marne and Meuse[78]. *Requiescant in pacem*[79].

Jack Richardson. 1915

---

[78]The Marne and the Meuse are rivers in France, both the scenes of early battles with great loss of life in the Great War.

[79]Latin - rest in peace.

MORE FROM MAY'S MEMOIRS

All this time Jack was training recruits and impatiently waiting for the call to service overseas. He was keenly interested in my more constructive work and looked forward to the early end to the war and a return to his own positive studies of literature. Quite unexpectedly his call came. On the evening of 16 March 1915 I was at home after a day's work in College when Jack called to say that he was leaving for France next morning, entraining at Waterloo Station for Southampton. His parents would see him off. Could I come too? So, on St.Patrick's Day, he went fortified by the great love we had been able to declare face to face for the last time.

Only long after did we learn that the whole London Division had been sent to France that day, no doubt in preparation for the Spring offensive. We only knew that casualties were now so heavy among infantry officers that an average life in the trenches was six weeks. Deeply grieving I went to Greycoat School and continued my normal work.

We wrote to each other every day. I sent him food and sketchbooks and his copy of Beowulf. He sent me a flower from No Man's Land or a sketch to keep me sharing something of this dreadful life. He was cheerful, daring, devoted, wholly involved in that miserable and distressing regime. It was about seven weeks later that the expected and dreaded message came: he had been killed while reconnoitering at night in front of his trench with his sergeant. Jack was an only child and the desolation of his parents was terrible to see. For myself, it seemed that I had frozen to death and there was only silence. Of course I went on with my work, grateful that it could take so much of my thought and gradually thaw my feelings. The worst of the effects came at night in my dreams, seeing him in all manner of' pain and distress. These dreams, sometimes repeated, continued for years.

Among the strange experiences of the inexplicable (or occult) that I shall have to relate in this history there is one that helped me to accept the devastating loss that had halted my capacity to feel. I was sitting alone, inwardly denouncing the folly and cruelty of man's treatment of his fellowmen, when suddenly I was aware of a warm tender strong presence reassuring me that all was well, that in this death there was a living, lasting reality. This seemed like Jack's actual voice; I accepted it as a new truth and was able to find new strength.

May Williams (née Larby)

NATURA MALIGNA[80] - A POEM BY JACK

Under a bough by the smooth flowing river,
In springtime all gleaming with sunset red,
Life is a garden of splendour, the Giver
One to whom thanks must ever be said.

After the sun comes the grey and the dark,
The wind sadly moans through scarcely leaved trees,
White mist for the river, and gloom in the park,
Silence unbroken broods over the leas.

Peace in the sunshine, but now desolation
Grips at the warmth and sleeping content.
The stillness of death expresses creation,
And strangles the fancies which daylight had sent.

So nature will smile in her sunbathed hours,
To mock at the wretch who screams in his pain,
Starvation and death she hides in flowers,
Murders in calm as in wind, storm and rain.

Jack Richardson. Trenches 1915

---

[80]Latin - malign, or malevolent nature.

POSTSCRIPT

A few years after her tragic loss May married another classics scholar, Richard Williams, and had four children; John, Elizabeth and Shirley. She continued her studies, became a successful mathematician, and travelled to mathematical conferences all over the world. As E. M. Williams she was awarded a C.B.E. for her contributions to mathematics in education and co-authored a textbook, 'Primary Mathematics Today', which is still in print and in use. May died in 1986 aged 91.

PART FIVE

ILLUSTRATIONS

May Larby aged about 20

Lt. John "Jack" Richardson

BLACKWOOD'S MAGAZINE

" Remains without a rival."
—DAILY MAIL.

" The only maga-
zine which every
lover of good
literature must
buy, borrow, or
steal at the be-
ginning of every
month."

Morning Post,
Sept. 13, 1912.

THE TIMES OF INDIA says:

"The other day the reviewer heard a man
remark that he never read 'Blackwood';
it clearly shows how blind people can be
when the very best lies under their eyes,
for not to read 'Blackwood' in these days
is to miss incomparably the most literary
and the most interesting of the monthly
magazines."

SPECTATOR.

"Of articles combining the picturesque
with the human interest, 'Maga' seems
to have an inexhaustible supply inaccess-
ible to any other periodical."

SATURDAY REVIEW.

"'Blackwood's' vitality is undiminished;
its individuality as marked as ever."

The magazine clipping referred to on page 32

Jack's telegram to May telling her of his embarkation to France

146

Jack and comrades on Salisbury Plain

Jack and comrades in the trenches

One of Jack's sketches, location unknown

Jack's sketch of the Mill, Old Melford, Suffolk

of no are very, very nervous & I think
they never dream of an attack — we
don't think they have sufficiently
strong numbers, either. They are
afraid all night long that it is we
who are going to advance & constantly
send up flares & use a search light
to make quite sure we're not creeping
up to their lines. When the time comes
I think it will be on our side that
the attacks begin. Yes, we go into the
same set of trenches each time — therein
lies the monotony of the work. As
to knowing my men — you will see that
I've got to know some, & I think all,
now, from my last note or two they're
all men of the 1/5th Co. 1. R.F. T.F. One must
write cypher to pass the Censor! My
dear, you must write to me just when
you want to — of course it can't be
too often; but I would have you write
only when you're in the mood — you have
so much to do, you mustn't have to sit

**One of Jack's letters as an example of
his handwriting**

151

Jack's sketch of the trenches

Jack's grave in Houplines cemetery, northern France